Stories of Love

C. Alan Ames

ISBN: 1-890137-44-8

Books Available in the U.S. from:

The 101 Foundation, Inc.
P.O. Box 151
Asbury, NJ 08802-0151
Phone: 908-689 8792
Fax: 908-689 1957
www.101foundation.com
email: 101@101foundation.com

and also in the following countries:

New Zealand
Patrick J. Clegg
P. O. Box 31495
Lower Hutt
New Zealand
Phone & Fax: 644 566 5786

Ireland
C & R Catholic Publishing
Templeshannon Quay
Enniscorthy, Co. Wexford
Ireland
Phone: 35-054 35295
Fax: 35-054 34341

England
Angelus Communications
22 Milbury Drive
Littleborough
Lancashire OL15 OBZ
England
Phone & Fax: 01706 372 674

Australia
Touch of Heaven
P. O. Box 85
Wembley
Western Australia 6014
Phone 089-275 6608
Fax: 61 89-382 4392

Australia—web: http://www.alanames.ws
Australia—email: alan@alanames.ws

1st printing, January, 2001 — 10,000 copies
printed in the U.S.A.
by the 101 Foundation, Inc.

This book is dedicated to Fr. Gerard Dickinson,
my spiritual director,
in thanks for all the help and guidance he has
given me in my seeking to do God's will,

...with special thanks to Tom and Carol.

INTRODUCTION

by C. Alan Ames

It has given me great joy to put into this book, some of the short stories given to me by the Lord, Our Lady, and the Saints.

Each one has touched my heart in a different way, with some bringing me a deep happiness, while others made me feel sad. However, in all of them, I found important lessons on how to live, to love, and to care for others.

When the stories were given, some I knew were real, as I would see them unfolding before me, and I came to understand that they had happened, or were happening at that moment, or may happen in the future. Other times, the stories were a means that the Lord was using to show people how His love relates to life on earth, and how people may need to change the way they live, if they want to have a happy and complete life.

As you read the messages, you will see some scriptural references, while others have none. This is because in the beginning, the Lord did not give me any references, but then in December 1995, the Lord began to do so.

When I am given a reference from Holy Scripture, it may be one or two lines, or only one or two words from a line. Sometimes two or three lines from different parts of Holy Scripture are combined to make the reference. The references at first were taken from either the Jerusalem or Douay-Rheims Bibles, but later, to avoid any confusion, my spiritual director (Fr. Gerard Dickinson, given to me in 1994 directly by Archbishop Barry J. Hickey, Archbishop of my diocese in Perth, Western Australia) and I, decided to use only the New American Bible for references.

I hope and pray that those who read this book will experience how God's deep love for mankind is there for all in a personal and intimate way, that His love is denied to no one, and that each life on earth can become another story of love written in the Heart of Jesus.

CONTENTS

1/5/96 — Jesus

IN THEIR INNOCENCE

A child took My hand as I walked through the town in which he lived. He sang and danced with joy as he walked with Me; his voice filled with love brought Me great happiness.

As we walked, more and more children came and joined in, all full of excitement, full of joy. I opened My heart to them all and filled them with God's love. In their innocence there was nothing to stop them being filled with it.

I wanted to stay with them and play, for it was a joy. I wanted to be with them in their happiness.

This is what I want for all mankind: to be as these children and have open hearts, so that I can fill them with My love and be with them always, enjoying friendship and love.

Matthew 18:2-4 — So He called a little child to Him and set the child in front of them. Then He said, "I tell you solemnly, unless you change and become like little children you will never enter the kingdom of Heaven."

IT WAS HE

My Mother one day took My hand in Hers and walked with Me to the markets. On the way we saw a man on the side of the road who was crippled and bent in pain. My dear Mother went and spoke to him to try and comfort him. He was in so much pain, it was difficult for him to answer but he begged for help. My Mother wiped his brow and held him in Her arms, and rocked him gently as he cried in pain.

Mother looked at Me with such sorrow in Her eyes it seemed Her heart would break. In Her eyes I could see Her asking Me to help. How could I refuse My Mother, whom I love so much?

I came to the man and placed My hand on his head, his pain was lifted and he stood up and danced for joy. Praising God he turned to Mother and kissed Her gently on the cheek and thanked Her for Her help.

Mother said, "Thank My Son, for it was He, not I, Who healed you." The man came and embraced Me and shouted his thanks to God.

In this action, My Mother showed that She will help lead those in need, in pain, in suffering; those who are lost, lead them to the love of God. Mother showed in Her humility that it is God who does all, but She also showed that I cannot refuse My Mother's requests for help, because I love Her so much.

Mankind should remember this, and ask My Mother to help.

2/2/96 — Jesus

I WOULD BE WAITING

As the whip bit into My back tearing My skin and the blood ran down My back, I felt the pain of all mankind's sins. As My knees gave way and I fell to the ground, the pain became so deep I wondered if I could go on; then I saw the hearts of My children and I knew I must.

As the soldiers abused Me, mocked Me, and beat Me, I looked into their souls and saw their true selves, and I forgave them.

As the crown tore My skin, each thorn became a reminder of how mankind had rejected God, and would continue to do so.

As the blood ran into My eyes, it became the blood of the little children denied their lives.

As I carried the cross, I carried the weight of all the sins ever committed.

As the nails entered My hands and feet, they became the sorrow that has been with mankind since it first sinned.

As they hung Me high upon the hill, the cross became the sign of God's love for all mankind.

As I took My last breath, I breathed God's forgiveness on all My children.

As the spear pierced My side, I flooded the world with God's mercy.

As I rose from the dead, I showed what awaits mankind...and as I ascended to Heaven, I promised mankind I would be waiting.

2/29/96 — Jesus

HEAVEN OPEN WIDE

One day a man came to Me and asked Me to explain Heaven. How could I put into words what he could never understand until he saw it for himself?

"Think of the happiest moment in your life and then imagine every moment like that, and realize that it does not compare to the joy in Heaven."

He looked at Me, saying, "Aren't there birds, trees, flowers, nice food, and enjoyment always?"

"Heaven," I answered, "does not compare to things of this earth, for it is far greater. The nicest things you have here do not compare to the spiritual rewards that await you there."

"I still cannot imagine it," he said.

"Instead of trying to find out what Heaven is like, try to find the way there, and when you do you will wonder why you spent so much time away from the path that leads you there."

"Where is that path? For I want to walk it," he said.

"I am the way. I am the only way. Through Me find the doors to Heaven open wide."

He looked. He did not understand, and so I said, "Live your life to God's commandments. Live your life full of love and helping others, but most of all live your life for God; then watch as the Son rises to light the path to Heaven."

He said, "I will pray, I will follow the commandments, and I will love God...and then maybe I will come to understand Your words."

"It is the same for all people. Without prayer, without love, and without living God's commandments, how can they expect to understand My words?

"In prayer find your heart opened to My love and see the path to Heaven clearly before you."

4/22/99 — God the Father

ALL THERE IN HARMONY

man was fishing one day and as he sat quietly staring into the water, he started to think about the fish in the water and what a wonderful creation they were. He thought how the water was there for them, and how all they needed to survive was in the water.

What an incredible bond between the fish, the water, and the food the fish ate. All there in harmony, all there without worrying about why, just accepting that it will continue to exist and continue to be there forever.

He wondered why mankind wasn't so trusting in creation; he came to see everything was here for man just as it was for the fish. Everything had always been here; it was only that he hadn't recognized this before.

He then started to think how wonderful is creation the way it is designed to supply all that is needed. Everything in creation working in unity to renew and continue what has been given. Then he thought: With such a complex system throughout creation, it is impossible that it is chance that caused this to happen, for there seemed to be a plan for everything and everything combined to keep creation alive. If it is so complex and is planned, he thought, then someone must have made it so. As everything is created to exist in harmony and peace, then Whoever created it must be benevolent and kind.

Then he started to understand this must be God, this must be the creator and that God supplies everything we need. He couldn't believe he had never seen this before because it is so obvious.

Mankind is like this man, he closes his eyes to what is obviously true, he closes his eyes to God's plan of creation, and closes his eyes to God. One day mankind's eyes will be opened and then he will wonder why he ignored what is so obvious.

4/30/96 — *Jesus*

BELIEVE IN MIRACLES

Two men walked the road one day discussing My life. One said, "I don't believe in Jesus being God's Son." The other said, "Well I do, and it is confirmed over and over in Holy Scripture." The first said, "Ah...yes, but that is written by those who wished to spread this belief. They may have made it up!"

In reply, the other said, "Jesus did live, did die, and is risen. So many witnesses proclaimed this after His death, even at the risk of persecution. Why would so many become martyrs for just a story?"

"They were deceived by clever men," said the first. "But," replied the second, "many of the first martyrs were clever and would have seen any deceit."

"They closed their eyes to the truth," said the first.

"The truth is Jesus," replied the other, "and He proved it over and over with so many miracles during and after His life on earth. So many cured, so many helped, and so many loved. Only God could do these things, not a man."

"I still don't believe," said the first.

"That is your choice, but when you die and you discover the truth, remember you were offered many chances to believe and you refused. Remember each time you refused to believe, and then know why Jesus refuses to ask the Father to forgive you. Your refusal is a denial of your Savior, and so you have no one to rescue you. It is like a drowning man refusing to accept the hand offered in help; he welcomes his own death. In your case, though, you welcome eternal damnation."

TRUE STRENGTH

There was a man who thought he was strong and could overcome all in his life. He relied upon himself and needed no other. One day he became ill and could no longer support himself. In his weakness, he discovered he did need others.

There was a man who thought of himself as weak, as unable to do anything unless God helped him. In his weakness he would call on God to give him the strength to help others.

One day the two met and the man who thought he was weak did all he could to help the other. He asked God for the strength and the compassion to do so, for he knew it was only God Who could give him the strength he needed to help another. The man who used to be strong accepted the help offered, and when he saw how much the weaker man did for him, how much he helped him, and how the weaker man never stopped caring for him, he wondered where the strength came from.

He asked the other, "How can you do so much? Where do you get the energy from?" The weaker man replied, "It is not I who has the strength to help you, but God, Who gives it to me as a gift to share with others."

"I used to think I was strong," said the first man, "but now I see you have the true strength of life, the strength that is found in God's love. How I envy you."

"Do not envy me," replied the other. "Just turn to God and you will find He has enough for everybody. He will give to you as He gives to me, if you truly want it."

Baruch 3:14 — Learn where is wisdom, where is strength and understanding, that you may know, at the same time, where are length of days and of life.

5/18/96 — God the Father

CONSIDER THE LILIES

 man one day sat looking at the lilies growing in a field. He wondered how they could grow so beautiful with no one to care for them; they just grew wild in the open.

He did not understand that God cares for them and gives them all they need to grow and become beautiful.

So it is with mankind. If people will open their hearts and believe that I will supply all they need, if they trust in Me, then they can grow and become the beautiful spirits they were created to be.

Matthew 6:28 — Consider the lilies.

6/18/96 — Jesus

WHY GIVE UP NOW?

One day a man walking along a road met another man on the same road coming the other way. "What is it like ahead?" asked the first. The other replied, "It gets harder to walk, the further you go along the path. I gave up; it was too hard," he said, looking dejected.

The first looked at him and said, "But you have come so far. Why give up now? The path behind us was difficult, but we overcame. Surely it is worth persevering for all the struggles you overcame to get this far!" The other said, "It is too difficult. I just don't have the strength left to go any further."

"Then take my hand and lean on me when you need to. I will help you get through the hard times ahead," said the first. "You would do that for me? You might not have enough strength for both of us. Go by yourself, I will only slow you down," replied the other.

"If I walk the road alone I will regret having left you behind. We are brothers. Come on, let's go together," said the first. They took each other's hands and walked on helping each other in hard times until they overcame and reached their destination.

This is how mankind should be, helping each other through difficult moments, looking on each other as brothers and sisters, and sharing their love as they walk the path to God in Heaven. A dream, many say, but it is a dream that can come true if mankind will just try.

6/29/96 — Jesus

UNDERSTANDING HEARTS

One day a man looked at his son and saw himself in his child. He saw his son making the mistakes he had made when he was young. He wanted his child to know that he understood some of the problems his son had, for the man had been through them also. The son would not listen, and the man was sad because he loved his child.

If the man looked at himself, he would see that he did not listen when he was young, so he was the same as his son is now. The man would also know that in time wisdom comes, and with that, a change of heart. He would know that his son would change, just as he did himself. He would know that God, in His mercy, will bring the understanding into hearts, that what they do is right or wrong. With that understanding many change for the better, as his son will, because God loves the man's son also, and this man's son, like his father, loves God, but does not know it at this time.

Jeremiah 23:17 — Peace will be yours.

<u>7/29/96 — *Jesus*</u>

EACH STEP

man was walking the road one day, and as he walked he counted his steps. He saw each step as a moment in time and wondered how many steps he would take before his life ended. As he thought on this, he came to understand that there are only a limited number of steps in his life and that he should make each step, each moment, the best he could, or it would be wasted.

Then he began to wonder what was the reason for his steps in life, for if there were no reason they would be worthless. As he thought, he began to see that if each moment was lived in the best way possible, then his existence would have a reason...and that would be to share his life, his love with others...and do the best for them that he could.

Thinking on this, he realized that if he was created to live in a good way, that he must have been created from goodness; and, if he lived as he was supposed to, then he would return to goodness. The more he thought on this, the more he saw that the reason for each step in life, each moment in life, was to grow in goodness, so that when his life came to an end, the goodness of his spirit would live on.

As he thought, he wondered...if all people were the same, then there must be a large body of goodness that those who had walked life correctly would go to. He realized this was Heaven, the place of goodness, the place created of good, the place created of God.

Then he understood God is goodness, and all goodness comes from God. Then he knew the reason for life is to grow in goodness, so we can return to God in Heaven, Who first created us from His goodness.

Isaiah 48:6 — Now I am revealing new things to you, things hidden and unknown to you.

8/11/96 — Jesus

MY FRIEND, FOR YOU

The day came for My sacrifice. As I sat in the Garden of Gethsemane seeing all of mankind's sins before Me, it broke My heart to see how men could stray so far from God. To see the harm they could do to each other and to themselves brought Me the deepest of pains, pain within My Spirit.

When My Father asked of Me and I saw My passion before Me, I did not know if I could go on; it seemed so much to give. Then Father was with Me, comforting Me, filling Me with the strength I would need to give. When Father asked, I could not refuse. I knew this must be, and so I accepted My Father's will.

I walked from the garden and into the embrace of betrayal. To see My friend Judas succumb to his weaknesses, to be seduced by evil, brought a deep sadness upon Me. Even the pain from the blows of those who beat Me did not hurt as much as seeing Judas destroy himself.

When I was paraded in front of the crowds and Pilate questioned Me, I did not deny, only confirm who I was, so that in times to come the world would know.

When I was tied to the post and the whip bit into My skin, I faltered a little, but then My love strengthened Me, as I saw how this would save so many. Each bite of the whip tore My skin and a pain burned deep within My body. I fell to My knees, as I could stand no longer under the beating whip. "When will it end?" I thought, as the pain intensified and I almost fainted. Then, as I thought I could take no more, it finished.

The soldiers dragged Me to a stool and placed a gown upon Me and a reed in My hand. They spat upon Me, beat Me, mocked Me, and abused Me. Then a crown was placed on My head, and as the thorns dug into My skin, I could not help but cry. The pain was so much. How cruel men can be. Each thorn reminded Me of the sins mankind committed and why this was needed.

A fist struck My face, and I swayed as I struggled to keep upright. Then I was taken to My cross, the sign for the world that God loves them. They put the cross upon My shoulder and led Me to Calvary. Carrying the cross I looked into the crowd and saw those who loved Me and those who hated Me; I carried the cross for all of them.

As I fell to the ground, the soldiers beat Me and beat Me. I thought, "Why is man so cruel?" On and on, I went climbing Calvary. Again I fell and a woman of love wiped the blood, sweat, and tears from My face. Still further to go. How can I go on? How can I do Father's will? I have not the strength. But within I find it, and My Father sends a helping hand. I look to My Mother who walks with Me and I see Her broken heart and I feel so sad. Mother smiles at Me and My heart is lifted a little from the pain.

We reach the top and My clothes are taken from Me, and as My back begins to bleed again I almost faint. They lay Me on the cross and I feel the nail enter My skin. The pain! How can I go on? I call from My heart to My Father as another and another nail bites into Me. All I feel is pain, all I feel is anguish, and all I feel is love.

Then they raise the cross and My body tears upon the nails. "Father, why have You deserted Me?" I cry, as the pain spreads throughout My entire body. "Father, forgive them for they know not what they do," I call, as I overcome the pain with the love of God.

A drink of bitterness makes Me even thirstier and fills Me with a feeling of sickness. "How much more, Father? Please take Me soon, I cannot go on," I ask from within.

I look to My Mother and see Her sorrow, Her suffering; a sweet child of God suffering so. My friend John is by Her side, and so I say, "Woman this is Your Son." I feel so weak. I know the time is near and I see My Father before Me, so I say, "Father, into Your hands I commend My soul." And then it is done.

In death mankind does not stop its rejection of God as a spear pierces My heart and lets My mercy flow from My side. Then I am in My

17.

Mother's arms, and as She strokes My hair, Her tears drop onto My skin. My sacrifice for you and for all; remind them, and bring My merciful love to them.

Matthew 26:61 — I have the power to destroy the temple of God and in three days build it up.

<u>*10/27/96 — God the Father*</u>

THE GIFT

man one day was offered a gift from a friend. Not wishing to offend his friend, even though he had no need of the gift, he accepted it. A short while later he met another who was in need of what he had received from his friend, and so the man gave it to the one in need. Afterwards, the man wondered if he had hurt his friend by giving away this gift.

One day, again he met his friend who knew that the gift had been passed on. The friend was happy that someone in need had been helped by his first action. The man was happy when his friend explained this to him, saying, "A gift given in love has no restrictions or expectations, only the hope that it can be useful. My gift was accepted in love so that makes me happy, but I am even happier that in love you opened your heart and shared my gift of love with another who needed it."

Always remember: give to those in need and always give in love, and when you receive gifts, see that they are there to be shared.

1/3/97 — Jesus

A BETTER FOOD

As a man sat eating his meal he thought how good the food was. He wondered if there could be a better food. One day he came to the Eucharist and thought, "If this really is God, show me." When he received Me within, I filled him with My love.

Now everyday he comes to the Eucharist and finds My love within it. He has come to understand that I am the true food of life, and no matter how delicious any food may be, it does not compare with the taste of Heaven found in Me.

Proverbs 9:5 — Come and eat my bread, drink the wine I have prepared.

4/20/97 — Jesus

THE ROAD

Walking one day a man came to a fork in the road. He looked, and said to himself, "If I go to the right it is a more difficult road, but I know it leads to home. If I go to the left it is an easier road, but I am uncertain to where it leads. Maybe it leads home, maybe it doesn't. Should I try it, for it is an easier looking road and it may be exciting discovering the unknown?"

Then he thought, "Well, at least on the path to the right I will get home, even if it is more difficult. I will go that way, for getting home is the reason for my journey, not excitement and seeking the unknown. I want to be with my family and safe at home."

Mankind has the same choice, one path that definitely leads home but may be more difficult to walk, or another that looks easy and exciting but leads to an uncertain end. Choose wisely, choose home, and choose safety, by choosing to walk the way of Jesus.

5/26/97 — Our Lady

TOGETHER WE CAN CELEBRATE

Ｔhere was a little boy who came and sat upon My lap one day. He looked up at Me with big round eyes and said, "Your Jesus is a kind man. He came and played with me." As I looked at this child, I said softly, with a smile, "Yes, Jesus is kind and He loves to play with little ones like you."

"He played a long time and it was fun," the boy said honestly. Then he laid his head against Me, saying, "You are nice, too. I like You." I stroked his hair and said, "I hope all will see Jesus as you do."

The boy began to fall asleep as I rocked gently back and forth, singing a Psalm quietly to him. The warmth and love I felt from this child filled My heart with joy, and with the singing of the Psalm, I offered this joy to God.

I saw then how Jesus had touched this boy's heart in a way that led him to Me, so that I could unite in love with the child and offer our love to God. How many people think that it is I that bring them to God, and forget that it is God that brings them to Me, so that together we can celebrate God's mercy.

Wisdom 16:21 — And the substance you gave showed your sweetness towards your children.

<u>9/6/97 — God the Father</u>

THE MOUNTAIN

One day a man climbed a mountain. As he climbed he began to lose his strength. Each step became a struggle, each breath painful. This man kept his eyes on the peak and persevered through all the pain to reach his goal. The closer he got to the top, the more he struggled, the more he hurt. At times he thought he could not go on, but within was a burning desire to get to the top that drove him on and on. Many times he slipped and almost fell from the mountain, but each time he pulled himself up and carried on his relentless climb.

Finally, with the top a few steps away he rested for a moment and as he did, a voice said, "Here, take my hand; let me help you." The man looked up surprised, as he saw another climber who had reached the top before him.

"Thank you, but how did you get here? I did not see you on the way up," replied the man. "Oh, I was climbing just a little ahead of you and I, too, like you, struggled to get here," said the climber.

"Yes, it is a hard climb," stated the man.

"But once you reach the top it is worth it, and you forget the pain and suffering it took to get here," said the climber, as the man came to the top and stood beside him looking out on the beauty before them. "Yes, it is worth the climb to see this," said the man.

They heard a noise below them and looked down to see another man climbing the mountain and struggling with this climb. Together they reached down, and said, "Here, let us help you with your climb. Come and join us at the top."

These men are like the saints in Heaven who have overcome the mountain of sin in the world, who, when they reach Heaven, offer their helping hand to those still climbing the same mountain they overcame. Mankind should not be too proud to accept the help offered, and should turn to the saints for their help in reaching the beauty of Heaven.

Wisdom 19:22 — Yes, Lord, you have made your people great and glorious. You have never failed to help them at any time or place.

7/27/97 — God the Father

NATURAL PART OF LIFE

A man one day sat looking in a mirror. All he could see before him were his faults...his gray hair, his balding, his overweight, his wrinkles, his aging, and his body becoming weaker. He did not understand this was his pride saying, "You are no longer perfect. What a disappointment you are."

He forgot that many of the faults he saw were not faults at all, but a natural part of life. He forgot this is what happens to all people; none can avoid it. He forgot to see the good in himself and in his life. Yes, these things were happening, but they were happening as they should.

Now, though, this man was letting them become a distraction in his life. Instead of leading a joyful life, he began to live one full of worry and concern over tomorrow. Nothing changed, he still got older, and his worrying prevented nothing, except his enjoying life as he should.

He died and went to the grave with his worries and having wasted much of his life. If only he had seen each moment for what it is—a treasure—and not worried about what was to come, he could have lived a joyful life as he was meant to.

Today, so many are like this man worrying about tomorrow and forgetting about today. If you make today important in your life, tomorrow can be a joy. If you make each moment one of love, tomorrow will be a treasure to enjoy, not a burden to suffer. If you make "now" God's, then eternity is yours in love.

Isaiah 7:9 — Unless your faith is firm you shall not be firm.
Matthew 12:32 — Either in this age or the age to come.

8/24/97 — Jesus

A DAY OF CELEBRATION

A man one day asked Me, "Will God forgive anything and anyone?"

I said to him, "In the love of God is total forgiveness, forgiveness for all sins and all people, if they truly repent."

"How can that be? For it would be unfair to those who have led a good life to see those who had not, forgiven and rewarded with eternal life in Heaven. Surely it would make the sacrifice of living to God's will not worthwhile, if those who did not were rewarded in the same way?" he questioned.

"In My Father's house are many mansions and there is room for all people. Those who have lived to God's will, will find their rewards are more than they could have ever imagined, and in their joy and love of God, would want everyone to share what they had. If they did not, they would not have been in Heaven, for there is no selfishness, no envy, no jealousy, in Heaven, only a wish to share the love of the Father with all of mankind," I replied.

"But that means you can sin in this life and repent at your last moment, and receive the rewards that the good do. What is the point of being good?" he asked.

"If you live a life of sin, you may not get the chance to repent, as your last moment might come before you know it. If you live a life of sin and say, "I will repent before I die," then this is no repentance, for true repentance comes from your heart, and then it is a heart that wants to sin no more. God knows who truly repents and who does not, and it is God Who judges all people and gives them the rewards they deserve.

"I tell you, it will be a day of celebration in Heaven every time a sinner repents...a celebration that says another soul is saved and is coming to Heaven. However, it will be a day of sadness when a good man begins to sin believing he will be able to repent and be saved, for this is a day a soul will be lost," I said, gently, to him.

He thought for a moment and said, "You are right, for how could a good man deny anyone salvation, and how could a good man believe he could sin and not have a price to pay. For if he thought this way, he would not be a good man at all."

"My friend, your heart is full of wisdom. Live to that, and you will live close to God," I stated, as I saw the goodness within him and the peace that had come to him with his new understanding of how the good should be...an understanding that all who proclaim to love God should seek.

Luke 1:50-51 — His mercy is from age to age to those who fear him. He has shown might with his arm, dispersed the arrogant of mind and heart.

10/26/97 — Our Lady

THE SAME PATH

One day a man was walking along a path. As he looked around him he could see beauty everywhere, in the plants, the trees, the sky, the birds, the animals, and in creation itself. Another man followed him walking the same path, but all this man could see was misery everywhere. He saw the clouds in the sky, and thought it would rain to spoil the day. He saw the fields around him, and thought what a waste of space. He saw the animals and birds, and thought what a meal they could make. He saw the trees, and thought they should be cut down for wood. He saw only how creation could be used for his benefit, and how creation would affect him. Before him, he saw no beauty, no love...he only saw his needs.

Two men walking the same path but seeing so differently, looking at the same things, with one seeing beauty and the other seeing self. This is how mankind is today, some walking the path of life and seeing God's beauty everywhere, while others walk it and only see self everywhere.

The path is the same, it is only how you view it that makes it different, and that makes your final destination different. Walk the path of beauty and love and find God. Walk the path of self and find misery.

Job 36:21 — Take heed not to turn to evil.

11/5/97 — Jesus

WHAT DO YOU BELIEVE?

One day, as I talked with a group of My followers, one of them asked Me, "Are You the Messiah?" In reply I asked of him, "What do you believe?" His reply was, "You are a good and holy man who lives to God's word, but I don't know if You are the Messiah or not."

I looked into his eyes, and said, "Look into your heart, see what it feels when you are close to Me, see how it cries out the answer to your question. Remove all worries, all cares, and all doubts, and just focus on what your heart says to you."

"My heart tells me to stay by Your side, for when You are not near, my heart hurts and longs to be near You," he replied, honestly. "But I still don't know the answer to my question."

"It is there, if you listen and if you allow your heart to guide you. This ache that you have within is the ache that all hearts have to be close to God. This feeling of never wanting to leave Me, is the feeling all hearts have in the true love of God. The thoughts that you have, that cover these directions from your heart, are thoughts that are there to hide the truth. Your answer is in your heart; it is plain to see but like many, you let your thoughts confuse you," I replied.

"How do I overcome them? They always seem to be there," he inquired, genuinely wanting to know how.

"Pray for the Holy Spirit to give you the gift to see. Pray to the Father to grace you with the knowledge you seek, and pray that the answer to your prayers is given to many others as well," I explained.

"Lord, You truly are wise in Your advice, for I see now I am only concerned about myself knowing the answer, while there are many others who need to know also," he said. As I looked at him, I smiled, saying, "It is when you seek to help others know the truth, that the truth becomes more obvious to you, for it is in the giving that you will receive."

"Yes, Lord, I understand now, and now I know You are the Messiah, for I can see my heart leaping for joy with Your words," he said, smiling happily.

"Take that joy to all you meet bringing sight to the hearts that are blind, so that they can see the truth of the word of God," I replied, seeing that this friend of Mine would do as I asked... just like I asked all My friends to do, but many were too blind to see this, and too blind to seek the sight they needed.

<u>*12/15/97 — St. Vincent de Paul*</u>

SOMETHING'S MISSING

boy went to his father and said, "Father when I grow up I want to be like you." The man looked at his son who was staring at him with eyes like saucers and eyes that were full of love and admiration. "Well then, my boy, you will need to learn your lessons and you will need to do as I do, but you will never be exactly the same as I am for you are unique, just as each person is."

"But I want to be the same as you," pleaded the boy.

"Well, if you want, you can be like me, but a little different. You see you may grow up to be much better than I am," replied the father with a smile. The boy was silent for a moment then said, "No one could be better than you."

"My son, it is in each person to achieve greatness in his life or not. Each person has a different quality that can make him great. For some, it is the talents in their hands. For others, their clever minds, and for others, the skills of life...but the one quality all have that can make them great, is the love in their hearts. All the talents, all the brains, and all the skills of life mean little without that love in your heart being the greatest gift in your life. All people are called to be great, and it is this love that shows who are the truly great," answered the father.

"You have a lot of love then," stated the boy matter-of-factly.

"No, my son I do not. At times I get angry, at times I argue, at times I do things I know I should not, and at times I regret what I have done. That is why I say you can be better than I. If you can control your anger, do not get into arguments, treat everyone with love, and try not to do bad things that you will regret later, then you will grow up to be a better man than I, and you will make me very happy," said the man to his son.

The boy came forward and put his arms around his father saying, "I think you are great."

"My child, the truly great are kind, loving, forgiving, and always helping others. Now that is not me, but I hope and pray one day it will be you," sighed the man.

"I will try, but you will always be great to me," said the boy, comfortingly.

"Promise me one thing, my son," asked the man.

"I will, I promise," said the eager boy.

"But, you do not know what it is yet!" exclaimed the father.

"I trust you," smiled the boy.

"Promise me in your life you will try to treat all people with love, and see each person as great."

"I will, I promise I will," said the son.

"Then I am a happy man," replied the father, as he ruffled his son's hair.

Then together they walked home for their meal.

This man was passing on to this son one of the greatest messages of life: to love and to treat all with respect, but he forgot the most important message of all, and that was to love God first and to see all goodness, all greatness, and all love come from Him. Without God in the lesson he was giving his son, there is a vacuum that waits to be filled, and so often it is filled with sin and with self.

All instruction on life, unless it contains God as the center of the message, is of little use, for all it teaches is about humanity and forgets divinity. This man was trying to teach his son to live in goodness, but without God in your life how can you truly live?

Psalms 81:13 — They followed their own designs.

<u>*4/15/98 — Jesus*</u>

THE PLAN OF CREATION

ne day a man looked at the sky and saw the clouds forming beautiful patterns. He wondered at the way they floated in the sky with such majesty. He thought about how they were made, and how the clouds brought water to the land. He thought to himself, "What a wonderful system has been created to bring rains to the lands."

He began to see part of the plan of creation and came to realize how, like the clouds, there are many other wonderful ways that combine, so that the world will thrive and so that life can continue. He began to see that there was an intricate network of systems in place for the survival of this world.

He reasoned that chance could maybe make one or two of these systems, but there were so many, and often so complicated, it was impossible for chance to be responsible. It surely must be planned. It then dawned on him that if it was planned someone had to plan it, and that some- one surely was a genius beyond our understanding and must have more power than we could ever imagine.

He then began to think of Holy Scripture and thought maybe it is true after all. Maybe God does exist, for who else could create such wonders? He began to look at a flower before him and all of a sudden realized the beauty in it and then realized that whoever created this flower had a heart of beauty and wanted to share his beauty in his creations.

This heart of beauty he thought, surely must be God, surely must be divine, for look at the life of the flower; obviously a life created by beautiful love. All of a sudden he understood God is real and God is the creator, and he wondered how he had been so blind before.

This is how it can be for all if they look with an open heart at creation. Then it will be impossible to deny the truth. The truth that is

33.

God the Creator, God the Father and God, Who is love.

Numbers 24:8 — It is God.

<u>*4/24/98 — Our Lady*</u>

I MISS YOU

s My Son Jesus sat at the table one day eating a meal with Me, He looked up at Me and smiled, saying, "Mother, Your meals are delicious. I miss Your food when I'm away." How happy that made Me feel inside to know that My Son appreciated what I did for Him.

Jesus calls to all people in the same way. He calls in appreciation of anything they do for Him, and He calls to those who are away from Him, saying, "I miss you."

Micah 6:2 — The plea of the Lord.

6/7/98 — Jesus

TRUE SIGHT

As I walked the road to Jerusalem with My disciples, we came upon a man who had been blind from birth. He was sitting at the side of the road talking to his companion, saying, "Even though I have never seen, I can feel beauty all around me. I can smell the freshness of creation in the air, and I can understand the wonder of each person when I touch them. I think my blindness has given me other ways to appreciate life and to enjoy each moment."

"But you miss so much not being able to see," replied his friend.

"Whatever I miss seeing, I am rewarded in other ways, for I think I discover more in life without sight than if I had it," said the blind man.

"You never saw your mother or father, surely you miss that?" asked the other.

"But I felt their touch, their warmth, their breath, their heartbeats, their love, and their joy. How many of the sighted are blind to these?" questioned the blind man.

"It's true," said the other, in amazement. "I can't remember those things in my parents. I've missed so much, how lucky you are to remember."

"Sometimes having the gift of sight can make you blind to life," stated the blind man.

As we paused listening to his words, I looked upon My disciples and smiled, as I said quietly to them, "There is a lesson for all in these words; you should think on them." Then we walked on in silence leaving a man with true sight behind.

Sirach 46:15 — And his words proved him true as a seer.

6/10/98 — Jesus

THE FISH HAS CAUGHT YOU

A man one day sat fishing and as he fished he thought about his life. He looked into the water and saw his face reflecting back at him. He looked and thought how his face had been as a child, then as a teenager, a young man, and now as an older man. He remembered how fresh and innocent he had looked when he was young and how today, with many lines upon his face and hair that had grayed, how tired and how burdened he looked.

He wished that he could have kept the freshness in his life that he had when he was young. He wished he still had that vitality and excitement for life. "Oh well," he thought, "that is for the young."

As he stared at his reflection, he gave a little smile and saw his face change to look a little more like it did when he was younger. As he sat there smiling, he thought, "If I can smile more, I will look a little less burdened." Still smiling he mused, "As I am smiling, I feel much happier than before. Maybe I should try to smile more often." Sitting there smiling and thinking, he began to feel a change happening within him. "Why did I let life weigh me down?" he said to himself, now delighted with the emotions he was experiencing.

Just then a priest walked by asking, "Have you caught anything?"

"No fish, Father," replied the smiling man.

"Why do you look so happy, then?" inquired the priest.

"Well, Father, I don't really know, except to say I discovered that, as I smile, I feel happy and I don't want that to stop."

"Oh," said the priest. "The Holy Spirit is touching you, my friend."

"What do you mean, Father?" asked the smiling man.

"Well, when the Spirit of God touches you, He brings joy and an understanding that it is only yourself that stops you enjoying the gift of life God gives you," replied the priest.

"It must be Him then, Father, for I can see clearly now that, if I am miserable it is by my own choice, and I do not want to be miserable any more," said the happy man.

"Well now that you know this, you should seek the Holy Spirit always in your life, and this joy you feel will stay with you," explained the priest.

"How, Father?" wondered the man.

"You should try to pray, to go to church, receive the Sacraments, and ask God to guide you. If you do this, you will be assured the Holy Spirit will stay with you," answered the priest.

"I will try, Father," responded the still smiling man. "I will try, as I do not want to go back to the miserable life I had before."

"Life is only miserable when you do not have God in it," said the priest, gently. "God brings peace, joy, security, and love into lives."

"Father, today's fishing is the best day's fishing I ever had, for even though I haven't caught any fish, I feel as if I have caught the biggest fish ever," said the amazed and smiling man.

"I think the fish has caught you, my friend," said the priest, "and the water of life has touched your soul."

As the priest walked away, he was also now smiling as he thought of the little white dove that sat on a branch above the man as the priest had spoken to him. "God is good," thought the priest, and at the same moment, the smiling fisherman thought, "God is good. I must know more; I feel so happy I never want this to end."

Little did he realize that now that he had found God, if he accepted God's offer of love, this joy would last for eternity. So it is for all people who at some time in their life are offered the love of God, and if they, too, accept that offer then a joy-filled eternal life is theirs.

Job 9:10 — Marvelous things beyond reckoning.

10/8/98 — Jesus

NO MATTER WHAT HAPPENS

A man one day struggled with the meaning of his life. He wondered what the future held and where it would lead him. He was uncertain of what he should do and where he should go. This all happened because he kept thinking of, and worrying about, himself. If he had trusted in God, that his life would be happy, no matter what happened, then he would have had no concerns, no fears, and no doubts.

It is the same for all people; they only need to trust in God to be secure in all things.

Psalms 119:165 — For them there is no stumbling block.

Jesus, I trust in You

MUMMY, I HAVE A BROTHER

little boy one day was wandering, lost and alone, uncertain of where to go. He felt as if he would never return to the security of his home and that he would be wandering forever. Then a gentle but firm hand took hold of his and he heard a loving voice, saying, "I will guide you home. Come, walk with Me." The boy looked up into the kind face of a bearded Man who was smiling gently down at him. The boy felt secure and happy and nodded in agreement. As the two walked on the boy asked, "Who are You?"

"I am your brother," replied the Man.

"I haven't got a brother. I am an only child," replied the boy confused.

"I am everyone's brother and no one is an only child, for they are all part of My family," replied the Man. The boy smiled, saying, "Well, it is nice to have You as my brother. What is Your name?"

"My name is Jesus," replied the man.

"Jesus," said the boy. "I have heard of You. My mother tells me stories about You. I didn't know You were real," stated the boy.

"Many do not know I exist, and it is because of this many are lost and alone. If only they believed in Me and put their hands in Mine, like you have done today, they would find they would never be alone again, and that they would never be lost along the way."

The boy smiled happily, saying, "I don't feel afraid anymore. I did when I was by myself."

"There is never anything to be afraid of, for I am with you always, watching over you and protecting you. All you need to do is believe in that," explained Jesus to the boy.

"I will, I will," said the boy joyfully.

Just then the boy's mother came into view calling for her son with a worried voice. The boy let go of Jesus' hand and ran to his mother shouting, "Mummy, I have a brother." The mother, with tears of relief hugged her son, happy to see him safe. "Mummy, Mummy, I have a brother," insisted the boy.

"No, my son, you are my only child and I love you," replied his parent.

"No, Mummy, look, here He is," said the boy, as he turned around and pointed down the path, only to see there was no one there. He looked a little confused as he said to his mother, "He was there. He was, Mummy."

"Yes, my son," said the woman, as she stroked her son's head soothingly.

"His name is Jesus and He told me He would be with me always and that He was my brother," said the boy, assuredly. The woman's eyes opened wide, as she said, "Jesus;" then she smiled softly saying, "Yes, He is your brother, isn't he?"

"Can you tell me more about Him?" asked the boy. The woman looked at her son saying, "I think it is time we both learned more about Him, as I have forgotten a lot."

"How could you forget about my brother?" asked the boy.

"I don't know; it just seemed to happen," replied the mother.

"Jesus said to me I would never be alone again," smiled the boy.

"Maybe it will be the same for you Mummy. Now that Daddy is in Heaven, maybe Jesus will be with you and you won't be lonely either."

The mother smiled, as she knew in her heart her son spoke the truth, and then she heard a soft voice in her head, saying, "I am always with you."

"Yes, my son, I think Jesus will be with both of us from now on," answered the woman. The two of them walked home hand in hand, talking happily of the Brother the mother had forgotten for a while. Walking next to them, even though they could not see Him, was the bearded man called Jesus, Who was always with them and always would be.

Psalms 118:7 — The Lord is with me as my helper.

11/22/98 — Jesus

HOPE FOR THE FUTURE

man one day walked hand in hand with his young son. As he looked down at his child, he wondered what would the future hold for him. He wondered if his son would be successful in life, successful in business, and successful in love.

He thought about the grandchildren his son may bring to him and his wife, and the children that his son's children would have also. The man smiled as he looked at his child holding onto his hand; he smiled with hope for the future.

Coming towards him he saw a couple walking with their child, and he thought about what the future would hold for this young one and his parents, too. As they passed, the couple smiled at him in greeting, and he returned their smile, saying, "You have a lovely son. I hope he brings you a lot of happiness in the future."

"Why, thank you," replied the husband, as the wife said, "And we hope the same for you." Then they carried on with their walk.

The man looked down at his son, saying, "It seems we all want the same things for our future lives. I wonder why we mess it up so much?"

"Daddy," replied the young boy, "I think sometimes people don't love and get angry with each other, and then they become unhappy. I always want to be happy, and if you and Mummy always love me, I will be," he said, smiling happily.

"We will never stop loving you," answered the father, as he embraced his son.

"And never stop loving all the other people, too, Daddy," reminded the son.

"That's the answer isn't it?" said the father, as he came to realize that if everyone lived in love, all their hopes for the future would be fulfilled.

"Come, and let's go home and tell Mummy we love her," said the man to his son, as he held his boy's hand a little tighter and walked the road home with new hope in his heart for the years ahead.

Psalms 106:3 — Happy those who do.

12/4/98 — Jesus

HE DOES HEAR

A man sitting in a church one day wondered if I could hear his prayers, if I was there with him, and if I would answer his prayers. Sitting there, nothing seemed to happen; there seemed to be no response to what he asked in prayer, and he started to think, "Maybe I am alone."

Disappointed, he left the church wondering... was he so bad that God didn't love him and wouldn't answer his prayers? As he walked with these thoughts filling his mind, he was overcome with despair and feelings that he may be offensive to God; otherwise, God would have answered his prayers, as God did for others.

A friend of his, who was a priest, was walking toward him, and as the man saw his friend he tried to avoid him, not wanting his friend to know of his despair. As he turned down a lane-way, trying to keep from meeting his friend, the man heard the priest calling him. He stopped and waited, trying to force a smile upon his face as the priest came closer.

"Were you trying to avoid me?" puffed the priest, a little out of breath after running to catch his friend.

"Uh...uh, not really Father," replied the man.

"What's the matter? You look as if the world has fallen on top of you," said the priest.

"It's nothing really. I was just lost in some thoughts," the man smiled weakly back.

"Well, I hope they are happy thoughts, not depressing ones. You know it's not unusual for people to start thinking about some little thing in their life they have done wrong. Then, next thing you know, they are drawn into thoughts of self-pity where they think God would not love them because the person is so bad. Soon it is easy for them to believe no one loves them, and next thing you know, the person is trapped into a depression which is often very hard to get out of," said the priest.

"Oh! It's not really that, Father. It's just that God doesn't seem to hear my prayers, or if He does, He doesn't answer them," stated the man.

"God always hears your prayers, but often the answer doesn't come in the way or at the time you expect," explained the priest. "Sometimes, however, prayers are not answered because what you ask for, or the reason for asking, is wrong, and so God does not answer. Sometimes the asking in prayers is a test of God's love for a person, as they think, 'If God loves me, He will give me this or that, and if He doesn't give it, then obviously God doesn't care for me.'

"Surely this is a wrong way to pray, for who are we to test God. Anything you ask for in prayer should be asked for in love, and asked for with acceptance of God's will in the answer, whatever it is…for only to accept the answer you want, is selfishness. How can you expect God to answer your selfishness? If He did, the selfishness may grow larger and larger. So sometimes it is better God doesn't answer prayers, for in doing so, He can often mould the person into what He wants him to be. This may seem painful, even very hard at times, but surely, if the end result is to change that person and to guide him onto the true path of salvation, it is worth it."

"So what you are saying is that by not seeming to answer prayers, God can, at times, lead us closer to Himself?" said the man.

"Yes, that can be the case," nodded the priest in agreement.

"Well, I'll be!" said the now smiling man. "You know, Father, I was asking God in prayer to show me a way of coming closer to Him, to show me He loved me, and to show me with a sign how I was to pray, as prayer was becoming very difficult. I even said, 'Give me a sign now Lord, so I know You are there, so I know You can hear me.' I was very discouraged when nothing happened, and I did begin to think God did not love me.

"That's why I looked as if the world had fallen on me. I thought I must be offensive to God, and I became really depressed, and all within a few minutes. Isn't God wonderful, though? For just when I was feeling my lowest, you came along with the answers to my prayers. You are right; you know God does do things in His way and in His time. I think I have learned a lesson today."

"And just as I said, sometimes God can mould you by not seeming to answer prayers, for He has today changed you a little, hasn't He?" smiled the priest.

"Yes, He certainly has," answered the now happy man. "Yes, He certainly has," he repeated, as he walked on with his friend, the priest, continuing to discuss and be amazed at how God had answered his prayers.

Proverbs 9:9 — Teach a just man and he advances in learning.

12/14/98 — Jesus

I MET A MAN

Walking the road to Jerusalem I met a man who seemed to be confused and lost. "Can I help?" I asked.

"Wh...what?" he stammered in reply.

"There seems to be something wrong. Is there anything I can do to help you?" I asked again.

"What...yes...uh...I don't know," said the man in a confused way. I went to him and placed My hand upon his shoulder, and as I did a peace came upon him.

He looked at Me, saying, "It's my son, I can't find him. He was playing by our house this morning but then he was gone. I don't know where. I have looked everywhere. I have been looking for hours. I fear he is dead. It will break his mother's heart. Oh, where can he be? He is only seven; we should have watched him more carefully."

"My friend, do not worry, your son is safe. At this moment he is at home with your wife," I said softly, but surely.

"He is at home! How do You know that?" asked the excited man. I looked into his eyes, and said, "Do you trust Me?" Looking back at Me, he said, "I don't know why, but yes, I do trust You. I know everything will be all right."

"Go home, My friend to your family," I suggested softly.

After saying a quick goodbye, the man ran as fast as he could along the road home. When he arrived there he rushed in the door excited and expectant, and there before him was his wife with their lost child in her arms.

"He is home," she sobbed, as she stroked the boy's hair.

"I knew he would be," said the husband, as he picked up his son and embraced him.

"How did you know?" asked the wife.

"I met a Man on the road, just as I was beginning to think our son was dead. He told me that our boy had come home, and I knew He spoke the truth; I had no doubt. It was as if my heart was filled with the knowledge that His words were the truth," explained the man.

"I wonder who He was?" mused the wife. "Did He say?" she asked.

"No, and I never asked," said the man. "But if I ever meet Him again I will thank Him, and from this day on I will say a prayer of thanks each day for Him."

"My husband, I will join you, for I feel in my heart I, too, have a lot to thank Him for," said the woman.

"Where was our son?" asked the man of his wife.

"He had wandered to the next village and a Man from there brought him home about an hour ago," the wife explained. "And, I think we should pray for this Man also," she suggested.

"What is His name?" asked the husband.

"I don't know, He didn't say," replied the wife.

The husband looked at his wife with an expectant expression. "What did He look like?"

"Well, He was about six feet, about 30 years old, dark hair and beard, beautiful blue eyes and the softest of voices, and when He spoke I felt at peace," explained the wife.

"It's the same Man! It is! I am sure of it! But how can it be an hour ago? He was with me on the road," said the man, a little confused.

"Daddy, Daddy," said the boy. "That Man told me He was here to help everyone, and He wanted to help me."

The husband looked at his wife saying, "Maybe He was an angel."

"Daddy, Daddy, I don't think He was an angel, He didn't have wings, and He told me His name was Jesus," said the boy, confidently.

"Jesus, the Prophet!" exclaimed the woman. "Some say He is the Messiah. Some say that He is the Son of God."

"Well, I believe He is, for His words were filled with truth," said the man with his eyes open wide, as he looked at his wife.

"My husband, so do I...so do I," she said in agreement, and then the two of them fell to their knees and began to pray in thanks to God. The boy joined in, and as a family they united in love, offering their prayers to God. At the end of the prayers, the son said, "He told me you would know who He was."

The father and mother embraced their child and each other, and the father said, "We do know, and now we will never forget."

As I carried on My journey, I prayed that many others would come to see the truth in My words, and like this family, accept them without doubt, and make Me part of their lives.

Isaiah 14:27 — His hand is stretched out.

49.

12/15/98 — Jesus

GOD'S BREATH

As a man looked in the sky and saw the clouds, he thought how beautiful they looked... like God's breath in the sky. Then, as he looked, he thought how true that was, and how from God's breath came the rain to bring moisture to the land. Then he thought how the rain was like God's tears, bringing God's love wherever they landed, and helping life come forth when they watered the ground. Then the man thought of the seeds that, with the help of the rains, grew into the plants that would feed the animals and humanity, to sustain their life.

Yes, he thought...God's breath and God's tears, bringing God's love to the world. How beautiful is God and how loving.

This man's thoughts were full of joy as his heart opened to the mystery of God's love in all things...a joy that is there for all who open their eyes to the gifts that God gives them in life, and the love He shows them in all things He has created.

Daniel 10:12 — To acquire understanding and humble yourself before God.

12/16/98 — Jesus

THE SOLDIER

A soldier was discussing with his friends the number of people he had killed. He spoke as if the people were objects, not human beings. He spoke with no emotion in his voice and discussed the subject matter-of-factly, as if it was only a job he was doing.

One of his friends smiled at him as he spoke; it was not a smile of humor or of support, it was a smile of pity.

"Don't you feel anything for the people you have killed?" asked the friend.

"No, they are nothing to me but the enemy," replied the soldier.

"Do you ever think about their families? They have mothers, wives, husbands, children. Like you, they have friends who love them. Doesn't it ever bother you that you are taking someone away from their loved ones?" asked the friend, with concern in his voice.

"No, not at all. It's kill or be killed. They are the enemy, and they mean little to me!" said the soldier in a firm voice.

"I suppose the enemy thinks the same about you then, and they would not care if you are taken from your loved ones," said the friend.

"That's war," stated the soldier.

"Well, surely that must say to you that war is wrong, for it takes away your respect for life?" asked the friend.

"I only respect my superiors and my fellow soldiers," said the soldier, with a steely look in his eye.

"How did you ever get like this? You used to be so gentle when you were younger," wondered the friend.

"There is no room for gentleness in this world. It gets you nowhere," said the soldier, with a tone that was filled with a suggested knowledge of life.

"And killing does?" asked the friend.

"Killing is necessary to defeat evil, so the good countries can triumph in this world," replied the soldier.

"But who decides which are the good or the bad? Surely that is subject to whatever influences a person has put upon them. I am sure your enemies think they are the good, just as you think you are. So who is it who decides which is good or bad? Sometimes it may be a government with an agenda of its own that conflicts with another government, and when an agreement cannot be reached between the two they often send their men to die. So it seems in many cases it is governments that decide what is right or what is wrong and it is the people who pay the price for their governments' decisions," suggested the friend.

The soldier stared at his friend, saying, "Well who else could we trust to tell us what is right or wrong?"

"If you rely on governments, you rely on people, and people can make mistakes, and governments' mistakes can often cost lives," said the friend.

"Well, who then should we listen to? Without governments there would be no order, no security, and no peace in the world," stated the soldier.

"Where is order, security, and peace? Look around the world and see so many conflicts, so much suffering, and so many in need. What security is that?"

The friend remained silent as the soldier sat thinking for a while, then he carried on.

"And it seems you have allowed yourself to be blinded to the true values of life, which are to respect each other, to care for each other, to love one another, and to treat each other as you would expect to be treated. When you lose these values, it is then you get drawn into accepting and believing so many of the wrongs that abound in the world, wrongs that cause the world to suffer."

The soldier looked at his friend, and said, "So all this fighting of wars is for nothing then?"

"War may at times seem like it is an answer to a problem, but in fact is a problem in itself," answered the friend.

"I wonder what the mother of the last person I killed is feeling with her son dead?" said the soldier with his head hung low.

"Think of all the mothers who have lost children in wars and think, is their suffering a price worth paying?" said the friend.

"What to do then?" said the soldier, with a shrug of his shoulders.

"The answer is to live to the Commandments of God, not of men. When people do this, there will be less suffering in the world and more love," suggested the friend.

"People will never do that; it's too hard," stated the soldier.

"Which is better: to try to love, or to live in hate and sin? If you try to love, life will become joy-filled. Surely it is worth making the effort, even though it may be harder to love, so that your life can be happy rather than sad," said the friend.

"But it would take everyone in the world to try to do that, to stop the problems we have," said a now despairing soldier.

"Yes, but it begins with you, and then the influence the change in your life has on others will help them change. First though, you must change and then that is when others will," answered the friend.

"I think I might not kill anymore," said the soldier. "And I think that war is not for me anymore, but I wonder what I will do?"

"Try to start loving and leave it in God's hands," said the friend.

"In God's hands. I never thought of that, but now maybe it is time I did and maybe it is time the world did," said the soldier with a peaceful smile on his face, as he began to feel the truth of life touching his heart...the truth he had forgotten: to love God and to love each other.

Isaiah 59:21 — From now on and forever.

12/23/98 — God the Father

A BEAUTIFUL SONG

man came across a dead bird on the side of the road. He looked down at the bird, feeling sad that such a beautiful creature had to die. He studied the colors of the bird and was deeply touched by their depth and natural beauty. "How sad," he thought, "that this bird will not be able to bring its majesty to the world anymore."

Just then, the man heard another bird singing in the trees, and looked up to see a similar bird sitting on a branch above him. The colors of this one were almost the same as the dead one, but because of the life in this bird, the colors seemed more vibrant. The man smiled as he thought, "Well, God gives us many gifts of beauty and now this dead bird's time has come, but here in this other bird, the gift of God's love continues."

He bent down and dug a little hole and placed the dead bird in it, saying, "Thank You, Lord, for this gift and for all the gifts You give to us."

As he was saying this, the bird in the tree was singing joyfully. The man thought to himself, "That bird is enjoying life, and I am sure this dead bird did the same when he lived. These birds seem to live each moment as a joy with little concern for the future. They live bringing God's gift in them wherever they go. Maybe that is how I should be, not so concerned for the future but living each moment for the gift it is, and trying to bring that gift of God's love in my life wherever I go."

He walked on noticing each bird in the trees around him and soaking in the beautiful songs they sang.

"From now on," he thought to himself, "I will sing a beautiful song from my soul to God wherever I go, and maybe, by the grace of God, I will bring joy to others, just as these birds are bringing joy to me."

With a smile on his face he continued his walk, a walk that would bring him closer to God, and a walk that would make his life, and the lives of those he met, more joyful.

Deuteronomy 32:3 — For I will sing the Lord's renown. Oh, proclaim the greatness of our God!

3/14/99 — God the Father

THE VICTOR

A man decided he wanted to be the best in the world at a game he played. He spent years and years training and practicing so that he could achieve his aim. His family became concerned with his single-minded attitude, as nothing else seemed to matter to the man. He had little time for family and friends, and even little time for God.

One day he had the opportunity to compete for the title of best in the world, and during the competition he gave his best, but he lost. Afterwards, he was dejected and felt as if his life was empty. However, the victor came to him saying, "It's not the end of the world. So you didn't win, but there is more to life than this."

The loser replied bitterly, "It's easy for you to say that; you won!"

"Yes, I did win, but I was prepared to lose, and if I did, I knew I had my family, my friends, and most of all, God in my life. This game is not that important. Yes, I enjoy it, and yes, I won...but if I had only this in my life I would be the loser," said the victor.

"I will be back and I will beat you!" snarled the loser.

"Thinking that way, you have lost already, I am sorry to say. Remember, also, no matter who is number one, always another will come along and take his title, and if that is all he has, then his life is over, as well as his reign as champion," smiled the victor gently.

"Well, I will be champion, and I don't care what it will cost. I want to be the best!" shouted the loser.

"You can never be a champion unless you put your life into perspective. All you will be is a bitter loser or a sad victor with few friends and a lonely life," suggested the victor.

"That will do for me," retorted the loser, with no thought in his mind except how he would come back to win this title.

"I hope you change. For me this was my last game. Now I will live my life and be happy thanking God for the skills He gave me," said the victor.

"But...but you are the champion. Are you going to give up now?" stuttered the loser.

"No, I am not giving up. I am just going to live my life as I should. This game is just that...a game, nothing else," said the victor.

"Well, I will be champion soon then," smiled the loser contentedly.

"Will you? You will always know I beat you so you will never truly feel the best!" said the victor.

The loser looked sadly at him, saying, "Yes, that's true, isn't it?"

The victor responded, "Don't let this game destroy you. See how unimportant in life it really is, and that there is much more to life than this. Do this, and you will find happiness in your life instead of misery."

"It's true, I do feel miserable most of the time," replied the loser. "I feel lonely as well."

"Well then, bring God and your family and friends into your life, and try to respect and help others. If you do this, you will find your life change for the better," explained the victor.

"I don't think I can do that. I have not done that for years and it seems so hard to do now," said a wondering man.

"Look how you have dedicated your life to this game and see how far you have come. Dedicate your life to thinking of God and others and you will succeed, just as you have had success in the game," suggested the victor.

"You are right, it has been hard training and giving so much to the game. If I can do that, then I can do anything. You're right, you know. I need more in my life!" exclaimed the now excited man, as it dawned on him what he had been missing.

"Well then, today you are the victor," said the champion, as he put his arm around the man encouragingly.

"We both are," replied the now happy man, as he walked towards his waiting family with a smile on his face.

"We all are," said the champion, pointing to the man's family. The man nodded in agreement as he went to his surprised but now happy family, and embraced them.

1 Peter 1:3 — A new birth to a living hope.

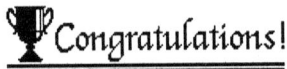 Congratulations!

7/11/99 — Jesus

THE PRAYER

man was huddled in a trench as bullets whined above in the air and bombs exploded all around. With him was his friend and companion, who was a soldier in the same unit.

"I never thought it would be like this," said the man nervously to his friend.

"No, neither did I," replied the other. "When I was joining the army it all seemed so exciting," he continued. "But there is nothing exciting about this; it is terrifying!"

"Yes, I also joined because it seemed like an adventure before me. Now I wish I was at home in peace and quiet there," answered the first man.

"Do you think we will survive this?" asked the friend.

"God willing," replied the man, as he looked up to the sky with an expression of hope on his face.

Just then, there was a large explosion nearby and a shower of dirt rained into the trench. Then another bomb exploded and more dirt filled the air. Both men sank lower down into the trench trying to make themselves as small as possible.

"You two get up!" snapped a sergeant, who had slid into the trench just as the last bomb exploded. The men lifted their heads and looked at the sergeant.

"Come on, I have a job for you!" snarled the sergeant impatiently.

"Wh...what is it Sarge?" asked the friend.

"You two miserable specimens are to try to silence the mortar that is on the other side of that hill," he said, as he looked over the top of the trench and pointed ahead.

"What, just the two of us?" asked the man.

"There is no one else to ask. The others are either dead or wounded; it is up to you two," replied the sergeant.

The two men began checking their weapons with automatic movements that hid their nervousness. "Besides, if you don't do it, we will all end up dead anyway," he said, as he shrugged his shoulders.

"Say a prayer for us, Sarge," asked the first man.

"Do you think that would help?" wondered the sergeant out loud.

"It couldn't do any harm," said the friend, with a worried look on his face.

"My mother told me, when I was leaving home to join up, that anytime I was in danger I should pray that God would take care of me, and it has worked until now," said the first man.

"Let's say a prayer together before we go," suggested the friend.

"Okay. I don't mind," said the battle-weary sergeant.

"What will we say?" asked the friend.

"Do you know the 'Our Father'?" questioned the first man.

"Sure," both the others answered, almost in unison. The first man began to pray out loud as the other two joined in.

As they prayed the noise of the battle faded and the only sound to be heard was their voices in prayer. Within a few moments from over the hill in the distance, they heard voices joining theirs in prayer. When they finished one "Our Father," they began another, and then another, and each time they could hear the voice of their enemies joining in. Eventually the prayers ended and there was a stillness in the air until the sergeant said to the two men, "Good luck," and indicated they should go and do their duty. Just as the men were about to climb out of the trench, a voice came from over the hill.

"Friends, listen to me." Then there was silence.

"My friends, listen to me," came the call again.

"We're listening," called out the sergeant with his hands cupped around his mouth to act as a speaker.

"Friends, if we can pray together, surely we do not need to hurt each other. Collect your wounded and leave. We will not fire on you," came the reply. The three in the trench looked at each other wondering if this could be true.

"Friends, we are Christians, too, and praying together has reminded us of that. Get your wounded and leave in peace. We will not harm you."

"Do you think they mean it?" asked the first man.

"I don't know," said the sergeant, "but it is worth the risk to see if they do," he said as he stood up out of the trench waving his hands in the air towards those now on the hill. They waved back enthusiastically.

"I think they mean it," said the amazed sergeant, as he walked forward to meet one of the enemy coming towards him. As they met, both men reached out and shook hands.

"Go in peace," said the enemy.

"You, too," said the smiling sergeant.

"Do you need help with your wounded?" asked the enemy soldier.

"Do you have some bandages and some field dressings?" asked the sergeant.

"I will be back in a minute," said the enemy soldier, as he turned and went back to the hill.

"Get the wounded together," said the sergeant to the other two. "I believe they are going to help us."

Soon a dozen wounded soldiers were gathered next to the three who were not injured. There was an uncertainty in the air as the sergeant said reassuringly, "I trust them; it will be all right."

"We will soon know," said the first man. "Look, here they come," he pointed towards the hill where about twenty to thirty enemy soldiers were coming towards them.

The enemy soldiers arrived with their hands full of combat dressings, and their hardened faces smiling gently and caringly at the wounded. The enemy soldier, who had come to greet the sergeant before, said out loud, "Until we heard you praying we were intent on killing you, but as we heard your prayers and joined in with you, we remembered that Jesus would not want us to kill each other. Instead, He would want us to love and help each other. So, here we are."

"Thank God for that, for I am sick of killing," said the first man.

"Me, too," said his friend. All the soldiers were agreeing and then embracing each other.

"Friendship is better than hatred," said one of the enemy soldiers out loud.

"Peace is better than war," said another.

"I would have never believed this could have happened, and all because of a prayer," stated the sergeant, with a happy look on his face.

"My mother was right; if you say a prayer, God will look after you," said the first man, as all around nodded in agreement.

After the wounded had been tended, the soldiers made their farewells and were about to part, when the leader of the enemy soldiers said out loud, "Keep us in your prayers, my friends, for we will keep you in ours, and maybe when this war is over we will all meet again."

The sergeant stepped forward saying, "We will pray every day for you, and we will do it in the confidence of knowing that by the power of prayer we will meet again. I didn't know how powerful prayer was until today, but now I and everyone in my unit know, and we will ask God that His power is used to protect you all."

"Till we meet again," smiled the enemy leader, and his soldiers joined in with similar farewells.

"Come on, let's pray as we go," said the sergeant to his men, as they moved off slowly because of the wounded.

"Wait until I tell my mother what happened here today," said the first man.

"When you tell her, thank her for me," said the sergeant. "I learned today never to forget to pray even in the most difficult times, and I learned never to forget to love even in the most trying times."

7/13/99 — God the Father

THE SMILE

A man one day said to his wife, "I love you, my dear, more each day. I don't know how it happens, but the love I have for you gets stronger every time I look at you."

His wife smiled back, as she replied contentedly, "That's nice dear, I love you, too."

The man stared at his wife's face for a few moments looking at the beauty of her smile. "I wish I could make you smile always," he said.

"You do dear, you do," answered the wife.

"What, even when we have our little disagreements?" asked the husband.

"Even when we disagree I am smiling within, because I know you love me," said the wife, reassuringly.

She sat thinking for a few minutes before she said, "You know the certainty that you have in your heart that God loves you, and when you think of that love how it makes you feel happy, and you know nothing can take that love from you?" queried the wife.

"Yes, my dear, I do," smiled back the husband as he thought about what his wife had just said.

"Well, within that certainty and happiness that is God's love, I place your love for me and my love for you, and I tell you, my husband, my soul is smiling in that love always."

The husband leaned over, embraced his wife and kissed her on the cheek saying, "That will be an eternal smile then."

"Come on! It's time to go!" said a harsh voice as the doors of the cell clattered open. "It's time for you to feed the lions," laughed one of the soldiers at the door before they entered and roughly dragged the husband and wife from the cell.

"Think of that love," whispered the wife to her husband, as they were pushed into the arena.

"I can think of nothing else," said the smiling and happy husband.

The soldiers left the arena and the cheering crowd became silent, as the growl of the lions could be heard as they ran up into the arena.

"My husband," smiled the wife, as she took his hand, "In God, I love you."

The husband looked at his wife, kissed her gently on the cheek, and said, "Be strong in His love, and soon we will be in Heaven together. I love you." Then he broke free from his wife's grasp and stood in front of her with his arms open wide, calling out, "Forgive them, Lord." He embraced the two lions that jumped upon him and turning his head to his wife, said, "I am thinking of that love." Then smiling, he fell to his knees as the animals began to devour him.

At that moment, the other lions took his wife, and as they did, she cried out, "In You Lord, we love."

The crowd was cheering wildly at the lions tearing the husband and wife to pieces. "What fools those Christians are," many said.

But at the same time all in Heaven, as they watched the two die, were praying fervently and crying, "What saints these Christians are." Then the joy of God filled eternity, as Jesus reached out and lifted the husband and wife into His arms, saying, "What love they have, what love."

7/16/99 — Our Lady

THANK YOU

As he waited in the hospital for news of the birth of his child and the well-being of his wife, the husband was very anxious. A nurse came and spoke to him reassuringly, "It will not be long now; do not worry, your wife is in good hands."

"I know, but it is difficult not to worry; she has had a difficult pregnancy," replied the man, with a worried look on his face. "And we have lost two children before."

"It will be all right," said the nurse, gently, as she put her arm around his shoulder, giving him a hug.

"It's in God's hands," shrugged the man.

"Well, there are no better hands for it to be in, are there?" asked the nurse.

"No, you're right," said the still anxious man.

"Whatever happens, it's His will; I know that," he continued. "But it is still hard."

"I know, I know," said the nurse, soothingly.

"Can I get you something to drink?" she asked.

"No, thank you. I don't think I could drink or eat anything," replied the man.

"Well, I will come back as soon as I hear anything," said the nurse, as she stood up to leave.

"Thank you," said the man, as he slipped back into his thoughts.

Several hours later, the now very concerned man was walking up and down in an agitated way, still having had no news of his wife and child. The nurse passed by, and, looking at the man, said in her mind, "Oh Lord, please let them be all right." Just then a doctor came to the man saying, "Sit down, please. I have something to tell you."

"Oh no, they are not dead, are they? Please, please don't tell me that...please," sobbed the man.

"No, no they are not dead, but there is a little problem," said the doctor.

"They are alive. Oh, thank You God, thank You," cried the now happy man. "What problem?" he asked, as the words sank in.

"Well you have a son; he was born 50 minutes ago," explained the doctor. "But..."

"But what?" asked the now uncertain man.

"He was born with a defect," said the doctor slowly, then paused.

"What sort of a defect?" demanded the father.

"There is a problem with his brain; it seems that it may not have developed properly, and because of that he may never walk or use his hands as he should. I'm sorry," stated the doctor, sadly.

"But he will live?" asked the father.

"Yes, he will," said the doctor.

"Thank God for that," said the man with a smile.

"How is my wife?" he asked.

"She is fine...a little tired, but otherwise okay," replied the doctor.

"Can I see them?" asked the smiling and excited man.

"Of course; follow me," directed the doctor, as he led the husband and now father into a room where his wife was in bed holding the baby boy.

When the wife saw her husband she began to cry, "I am sorry, I am sorry. I couldn't give you a healthy baby, I am sorry," she was sobbing and sobbing as the husband came to her smiling.

Reaching out he embraced his wife and his son. "You have nothing to be sorry about; you should be happy we have a son...a son that God gave to us. What a gift!" he said, lovingly.

"But he will never be normal," sobbed the wife.

"That is the way God gave him, and we must be grateful for that," answered the husband, with a certainty in his voice.

"Oh my husband, I love you, and I am thankful to God that He brought such a good man into my life," smiled the wife, as she strained her neck to lift her head and kiss her husband on the cheek. The husband leaned across her and kissed his sleeping son, saying, "And we must never stop thanking God for our son, either."

The doctor went out into the corridor shaking his head, "What is it, doctor?" asked the nurse, who had comforted the man earlier.

"They have a deformed baby and they are thanking God for it. I can't believe it," he answered.

"Why not?" inquired the nurse.

"Well, the child is deformed. I thought they would be angry with God...not thanking Him."

At that moment the father came from the room, went over to the doctor and shook his hand, saying, "Thank you, doctor, thank you." Then he rushed off to find a telephone to call his family.

"See what I mean?" whispered the doctor.

The nurse looked at the doctor, and said, "These people see the value of life and what a wonderful gift it is from God. They do not look at what may be wrong in the child, they see what is right, and it is right that this child lives and has a happy and loving family, as all children deserve regardless of appearance, of deformities, or of the extra work a child may bring to its parents. All children are a gift of God's love, and none deserve to be treated as if they are not."

The doctor was silent for a moment, then said, "I suppose you're right; this job has made me a little callous." He left to carry on with his duties.

The nurse smiled and went off to visit the child-caring center, where her own daughter was playing. She entered the room to her smiling daughter, who came running towards the nurse with her arms open wide, wanting an embrace.

"Mummy," called the daughter happily, as she sank into her mother's arms. The nurse began to cry as she felt the love of her little daughter touch her heart, and she knew that the Downs Syndrome her child had did not stop her love...it enhanced it.

7/20/99 — God the Father

JUST LIKE YOURS

As the people gathered for the wedding, the bride was nervously preparing herself in her room for the ceremony that lay ahead.

"Mom, were you nervous on your wedding day?" she asked of her mother, who was helping her dress.

"Of course I was, dear. I was nervous and I was very excited," replied the mother, with a voice that said I know what you are going through.

"I want my marriage to be like yours and Dad's," smiled the daughter, hopefully.

"It can be, if you want it to be; you just have to work at it," explained the mother.

"Mom, so many marriages end in divorce today. I don't want that to happen to mine," said the daughter.

"Marriage is a wonderful gift from God, given in love, and it should be received and lived in love. If you remember this, especially in the difficult moments you will have, then your marriage will last and it will grow stronger with time. It is when people forget this that they run the risk of a marriage break-down," replied the mother.

"I know there will be hard times Mom, but I really love him and I think we can come through these, just as you and Dad have," stated the daughter.

"Of course you can. Everyone can if they try. Unfortunately, many today find it so easy to walk away from their marriages when they have problems, rather than making the effort to over-come them. Your father and I have had our trying times, but, by the grace of God, we have come through them and we are happy," said the mother, with a look of contentment on her face.

"When you have a problem," she continued, "you must talk about it and clear the air. Don't try to hide it, for it won't go away. When you do talk, remember why you got married; remember the love you have for each other, and remember the sacred vow you have made before God, for that is what marriage is. Whenever your father and I would argue, I would go and pray for God's help and you know your father always joined me in prayer, and then the problems didn't seem so big and we got on with loving each other, as people are supposed to in marriage."

"Thanks, Mom; I will remember anytime we have troubles to do as you and Dad did. I'll pray, too, but I don't know if my husband will join me, as Dad did with you," she said, a little unsure.

"Your father never used to at first, but when he saw how peaceful I was in prayer, he soon joined in. You wait and see, God has a wonderful way of bringing people to Him, and I'm sure He will touch your husband through your prayers," said the mother, reassuringly.

The daughter smiled in hope, unaware that at that moment in her future husband's house, his father was saying to him, "Remember, it is God and prayer that has kept your mother's and my marriage strong. It will be the same for you; don't forget that."

"I won't, Dad, because I want my marriage to be as good as yours is," replied the son, hoping in his heart that his new wife would be prepared to join him in his prayers.

"If you give your marriage to God, Son, it will be. It will be," said the father with certainty, as he patted his son on the back.

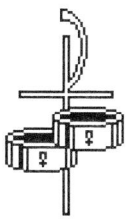

<u>*7/25/99 — Our Lady*</u>

OH NO!

young man was speaking to his parents, saying, "I have made a decision about my future, and I would like to share it with you." He paused as he looked at his parents' faces, which had a look of apprehension on them.

"What is it, Son?" asked the father, breaking the silence.

"I want to be a priest," replied the son, firmly.

"A priest! Oh no!" exclaimed the mother, as she put her hands to her face.

"Yes, Mum, a priest," nodded the young man, with certainty in his eyes.

"But you are so talented, there are many other things you could do...good jobs with lots of money. You do not want to waste your life in the Church, and what about children? If you become a priest, I won't have any grandchildren," wailed the mother in despair.

"Have you thought this over, Son?" asked the father. "Do you know the sacrifices you will have to make...how hard it will be?"

"Dad, I have been thinking of almost nothing else for a long time now, but I am certain I want to be a priest," replied the young man.

"Why...why...why?" asked the mother, as she shook her head in disbelief. "Whatever has gotten into you to make you want this?"

"Mom, Dad, I know it is difficult for you to understand at the moment, and I know you wanted me to have a family, but that is not what I want. Yes, for a while I thought it may be, but I always knew deep inside of me there was something else I was meant to do with my life. With the work I do, I have always felt empty, as if something was missing.

"With women, I see them all as sisters I love; nothing else. It is only since I decided on the priesthood that my emptiness has gone, and I know that this is what I am called to.

"A family, yes I will have one—it is the family of God; it is every person on earth. No, in a physical sense I will not have children of my own, but every child I see I will treat as if it is mine, and I will do my best to bring God's love to every child. You ask what has gotten into me? Well, it was in me always...it is the love of God.

"I know now that God's love is the driving force in my life. I know now that God's love makes me feel complete. I know now that I need nothing in my life but God's love, because in His love I will be given all that I need. I feel His love so strongly inside of me, and as I feel it, I want more. As I feel it, I just want to call out to God that I love Him. I just want to please Him in all I do. I just want to serve Him in bringing others to His love.

"This is the meaning of life for me. I know it, I believe it, and I want to live it. To me this is the greatest gift of life and now, through the priesthood and by the grace of God, maybe I can help others to find this gift also."

The young man stopped speaking and looked at his speechless mother and his now smiling father. "Son, you have my blessing," said the father. "Each word you spoke touched my heart, and I know you will make a good priest," he continued. The mother remained silent with a tear rolling down her cheek, until she said, "My son, a priest," Then she came to her son and embraced him, kissing his forehead and stroking his hair. "If that is what you want, I am happy for you," she said.

"It is, Mom. It is," said the young man, gently.

Then the mother looked at her son, and said, "Well, if God has called you, I can't stand in your way. Come on; let's say a prayer together and thank God for choosing a priest from this family." Then, as they joined in prayer together, all three of them felt within their hearts God's love filling them. The father said out loud, "You are right, my Son, and I know you will be a good priest. Thank God."

Then the mother, filled with the Spirit cried out, "It's true, it's true. How wonderful; my son is going to serve God in His Church. Oh, praise God!" The future priest smiled, and said within his heart, "Thank You, Lord. I knew You would bring them to understand."

Now all three prayed fervently and confidently, asking God that this gift of the priesthood would be one to bring glory to God.

7/26/99 — Jesus

LOVE MADE HIM HAPPY

grandmother one day was looking after her three grandchildren...all of them boys. The eldest was seven, the second eldest five, and the youngest just a year old. The youngest was in his grandmother's arms, as she sat and told a story to all three of them.

"One day," she said, "a baby was born in a stable because His parent and guardian had found no where to stay. It was a cold night, and in the stable there was little warmth, except that which came from the animals in there."

"Why did they have nowhere to stay, Grandma? Were they poor?" asked the eldest.

"Yes, they were. poor, but all the places they asked to stay would not let them in, because each one was full of visitors that night. The king had called all the people together so they could be counted and there was not enough room for everyone," explained the grandmother.

"Was the baby cold?" asked the wide-eyed three-year-old.

"No, He wasn't because His family had made a wooden manger into a warm bed for Him," answered the grandmother.

"What's a manger?" asked the inquiring seven-year-old.

"A manger is what was used in olden days to feed animals," she replied.

"Was there any food in the manger when the baby was put into it?" asked the boy, with a screwed up face.

"No, of course not," said the woman, as she smiled and shook her head.

"Grandma, did the animals try to eat Him?" said a curious five-year-old, as he imagined the animals trying to eat the baby.

"No, the animals loved Him, and anyway His family was watching over Him," responded the still smiling grandmother.

"Was He frightened?" asked the seven-year-old.

"I think, like your young brother here, He would have spent most of His time sleeping," she said, as she looked at the youngest asleep in her arms.

"When I was a baby I used to sleep a lot," said the five-year-old importantly, as he tried to look a lot older.

"I am glad He didn't get eaten," said the oldest boy.

"So am I," joined in the five-year-old.

"Well, soon three kings came to visit the baby boy, and each of them brought Him a gift. The kings had come, because a star had shone its light on the baby." The grandmother paused as she looked at the two boys staring intently at her waiting for the next words. "And the kings had followed that light because they knew the One the star shone above, was the King of Kings."

"But you said He was poor; kings are rich," said a confused seven-year-old.

"Yes, He was poor, but that did not stop Him being a King. Not all kings have lots of money and gold. This baby had more than that, He had more than all the kings in the world put together," explained the grandmother.

"Wow!" said both the boys together.

"This baby boy had all the treasures of God, for He is the Son of God and His name is Jesus. He was, and is, the King of Heaven as well as all of the earth, and He came down from Heaven to show the people that God loved them."

"Grandma, if He was so rich, why was Baby Jesus born in a cold stable?" asked a still confused seven-year-old.

"He did that to show everyone that God loved even the poorest, and that money and gold did not make any difference in God's love of people. If He came as a poor baby, then the poor would know that they were important to God, also," explained the grandmother.

"Did He grow up to be rich?" asked the older boy.

"No, He stayed poor. He never really had any money," replied the grandmother.

"Did He marry a princess?" asked the five-year-old.

"No, He didn't marry," smiled the woman.

"Grandma, if He didn't have any money, and He didn't marry a princess, and He was very poor, He must have been very sad," stated the older boy.

"Remember, I said He had all the treasure of Heaven? Well, He didn't need anything else. The treasure of Heaven is love, happiness, and joy. What more did He need?" asked the woman.

"He might need some money to buy things," said the older boy.

"He might want some toys," agreed the younger.

"What do you boys like better, to be loved by your Mom and Dad, or to have some money in your hand?"

"To be loved by Mom and Dad," they called out together.

"Do you prefer to play with your toys, or to be cuddled by Mom and Dad?" asked the grandma.

"Cuddled by Mom and Dad," responded the boys together.

"See, love is better than things then, isn't it?" asked the woman.

"Umm...yes," answered the boys.

"And things like money and toys can be lost or broken, but true love never can," said the woman, as the one-year-old began to stir in her arms. "And to me true love is the biggest treasure of all. This is what Jesus has, for He is God's Son, and God is true love."

"And to me!" said the five-year-old, who then said, "I want what Baby Jesus has."

"And me!" said the seven-year-old.

"Well, you can have that, if you remember how Jesus did not want lots of gold and silver, and how it was love that made Him happy. If you try and do the same, then Baby Jesus will bring His love into your life and you will be happy," said the grandmother with certainty, and then she turned to kiss the one-year-old on the cheek, saying, "And you, too."

Then she embraced all three of them saying a silent prayer in her heart that her grandchildren would never forget the love of Jesus in their lives, and never lose the happiness that comes with it.

8/21/99 — Holy Spirit

WHAT AN EXCITING BOOK

man sat reading a book that was an adventure story. As he read, in his mind it was as if the story was alive and he was part of it. The man was reluctant to put the book down and was determined to finish it, so he would know how it would end. When his wife brought him a drink or some food, he paid little attention to her and continued to read.

"That must be a good book," said the man's wife, as she sat in a chair opposite him. The man just grunted and nodded in agreement.

"You have hardly said a word to me since you started to read it," said the frustrated wife.

"Sorry," replied the man, as he lifted his eyes over the top of the book to look at his wife. "I've nearly finished," he said, as he looked into it again and continued to read.

"I'm going to bed; I have had enough of this," snorted the wife, as she rose to leave the room.

"Yes...yes," replied the husband impatiently, as he continued to read. "I'll be there soon," he said, with a tone that implied he really did not mean what he said.

The wife went off to bed, deciding to read a book of her own for a little while before she slept. She reached over to her bedside table and picked up a copy of the Bible that lay there and began to read it.

Some hours later her husband came into the bedroom saying out loud, as he stretched out his hands above his head, "I've finished it, dear. What an exciting book that was; I couldn't put it down."

"Sssh," said the woman without looking at her husband, but still looking at the open Bible in her hands.

"Oh, sorry; you are reading," said an apologetic husband. "Will you be long?" he asked.

"I don't know. This book is very exciting, I can't put it down," replied the woman.

"Oh, I see; you're getting your own back," said the husband, as he shook his head.

"No...no, I am not. This book is different, truly.
Sssh, let me read," pleaded the woman.

"But it's only the Bible...nice stories, but there
is nothing exciting in there," said the man in a
derogatory way.

"Sssh," said the wife loudly.

The man went and washed, then got changed for
bed, and returned to the bedroom where his wife
still had her head buried in the Bible.

"Which part are you reading that is so exciting?"
asked the now frustrated man.

"I have just finished the Crucifixion, and now
Jesus is breathing the Holy Spirit into the apostles.
It's amazing; I feel as if I am there. I saw Jesus
on the Cross dying, and as He did, He looked at
me. I couldn't stop crying. Now I feel His breath
touching me, and my heart is racing. I feel so
excited, so happy, and as if Jesus is filling me
now at this very moment with His Holy Spirit, just
as He did with the apostles," explained the wife,
with her eyes open wide and a big smile on her
face. "This is the best book I have ever read,"
said the wife excitedly. "I never knew it could be
like this. The Bible is truly alive. Now I know
what they talk about at Church on Sundays."

The husband looked at the woman he loved and
knew something special had happened, for in the
30 years they had been married, she had never
been like this. The smiling woman said to him,
"Come and read a little; you will see, too."

"It's not my type of book, dear. I like adven-
tures," he replied.

"Believe me, every passage in this book is an
adventure, an adventure of love," said the woman,
as she reached out to take her husband's hand
and pull him to sit beside her on the bed.

"Close your eyes and I will read you a little,"
she said softly. The man did so, and as his wife

began to speak her voice seemed different. Each word seemed so gentle, so soft, so loving, so filling, and yes, so exciting. Now, as he saw in her words Jesus before him, his heart began to race. Now he was waiting on every word, he could hardly sit still as he saw in his mind a beautiful white dove fly into his heart and he felt as if he was being lifted into the air. He opened his eyes and looked at his wife, who was crying with joy, and he, too, began to cry for the same reason.

"I love God!" cried the wife.

"So do I," answered the husband, with amazement in his voice.

"See, I told you it was the best book," said the wife, as she reached out and embraced her husband.

"It is the greatest of all time," agreed the husband.

Then, as he raised one hand in the air, "The greatest!" he shouted. Together they lay back holding the Bible between them and smiling at each other.

"I feel my love for you in a new way," said the man to his wife.

"Me, too," she replied, knowing exactly what he meant. Together they lay there looking at each other, holding tightly onto the Bible, not wanting to let go of it, for now they knew God was there with them in His holy and living Word. Slowly, as they drifted to sleep, the Bible fell between them and as the pages opened, a beautiful white dove flew out from it and settled on the headboard above them. The dove looked down upon them smiling at the two who had discovered true love, true life, and true adventure in the greatest book of all...The Living Word of God.

I OFFER IT ALL

woman was busily cleaning her house, and as she did so, she prayed in her mind, offering her work as a prayer to God. The woman did not like cleaning; she would have been happy if she could have done something else and left this job for others to do. However, she knew her husband, who worked all day, would be the only other person who may do it. Because her three children were too young, she couldn't leave it for him, as he needed his rest so he could be able to work. So, in the love of her family, she did the cleaning, and in the love of God, she offered this sacrifice she made, so that others may be graced by God in some way.

The woman smiled as she thought about friends that did not have children and who could, if they wanted, get a maid to do the housework. The woman thought about the difficulties she had in life, but even with all these, she knew she would not change places with her friends, because the woman was loved by her husband and she loved him, and together they had beautiful children whom they both loved. In her heart, she knew that God had made it this way. God had graced her with such a loving family, and to her that was a great sign of God's love for her.

The woman began to sing a hymn out loud, thanking God for His generosity to her, and as she did, her heart seemed to be filled with happiness. It felt as if it would burst. She sang louder and louder, trying to put all the happiness she was feeling in her heart at that moment into each word. Now every action she did in her cleaning made her feel even happier, and she began to time the movements with the words of the hymns she was singing.

Soon, her work was finished and she then fell to her knees in joy, calling out, "Thank You, God. I love You. Thank You for loving me and showing me that even in what we do not like doing, the joy of Your love is to be found, when it is offered to You as a true sacrifice and prayer of love. Thank You, Lord!" she cried out loud.

Just then her three children came into the room rubbing their eyes, as they had just woken from their afternoon nap.

"Mummy," they called in unison, as the three of them ran towards her with their arms outstretched; she embraced all three and kissed each one lovingly. Then the woman looked upward saying, "Thank You, Lord."

The children saw what their mother did and also looked upward, imitating her and saying in unison, "Thank You, Lord." The mother knelt there embracing her children and smiling happily as she said over and over, "Thank You, Lord. I am so blessed."

At that moment in his office, the woman's husband had his Rosary in one hand. He was praying the Joyful Mysteries for his wife, offering it to God that today would be a happy day for her. He also offered to God every figure and word he wrote down with his other hand as a part of his work, as a prayer for his wife. Inside he felt happy and he felt secure knowing that his family's lives were in God's hands.

"No better place for them to be," he thought, as he continued praying, working, and smiling.

"How can you be so happy all the time?" asked a colleague who shared the office. "This work is so tedious; it's boring and it drives me crazy. If it wasn't for the money, I would have quit ages ago."

"Well, I have a family to support; I also need the money, and this is the work I do," stated the husband, still smiling.

"Yes, but you enjoy it!" exclaimed the colleague.

"I never used to, but I started praying in my work," said the husband, as he lifted up the hand with the Rosary in it.

"See, and I offer all the work I do as a prayer to God for my wife and children. Since I started to do that, I started to enjoy the work, because now I see it as a way of helping my family through the graces God grants. As I pray, I sometimes see myself with my family, not here, and that makes me happy. Just a moment ago in my mind I saw my wife embracing the kids and they all looked so joyful. That made me feel good. You should try it," suggested the husband to his colleague.

"Maybe I will," replied the man, thinking to himself, "This guy is nuts."

The colleague returned to his desk and continued his work which seemed to get heavier and heavier with each word he wrote. He looked up at the still-smiling man nearby, who looked back at him, and said, "Try it!"

Then, surprised with himself, the colleague began to pray in his mind as he worked. Within a short while, he was smiling as he worked and he couldn't believe how good he felt. The colleague looked up at the husband and smiled to him, saying, "Thank you, it works."

At that moment, the superior walked into the office and saw the two smiling men. "Hey, it's great to see two happy workers. I know this job is a little monotonous, so every day I pray to God you will not get too frustrated with it. Seems like my prayers are being answered," he said, happily. He didn't know how true his words were, and how it was not only his prayers, but also the prayers of the sacrificing wife that were being answered.

 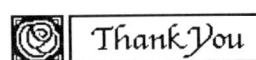 

8/26/99 — Jesus

WHAT SENTENCE?

As the man stood before the judge who was about to sentence him, he pleaded for leniency.

"I was confused by the drugs I had taken. If I were in my right mind, I wouldn't have done it. I am truly sorry for the hurt I have caused, and now that I have been drug-free for some months, I see how stupid I was. Sir, I know I have done wrong, but at that time, my only desire was to get drugs regardless of how I achieved that. I am sorry, and I hope that I can in some way make up to society for the wrong I have committed."

The judge looked squarely in the man's eyes for a moment, then knew in his heart that he was about to condemn this man to death. As he opened his mouth to speak, all of a sudden in the convicted man before him he saw his oldest son; then the man changed to be his daughter and then his youngest son. The judge rubbed his eyes and looked again at the man in disbelief, but again he saw each of his children in the convicted man before him. Then inside his head the judge heard a voice saying, "What would you do if it were your children before you? If this man had the advantages your children have had in life, he probably would not be here, but if your children had the disadvantages this man has had in his life, they probably would be here."

The judge sat silently, still looking at the convicted man.

"Your Honor, are you all right?" asked the prosecutor who was eager to hear the sentence, hoping it would be the death penalty he had asked for.

"Yes, I am fine. I am just considering my sentence a little longer," replied the judge.

"This man is part of your family and you should treat him as such," continued the voice inside the judge's head. "He has made a serious mistake in his life, but he deserves the chance to make amends for it, both for society and for his soul. Yes, he has killed, but if you kill him, are you any different from him? The only difference will be that you in your mind will justify your cold and calculated act, while this man, who was confused and unbalanced under the influence of evil, is full of remorse for what he has done and will never justify to himself the terrible crime he has committed. Who is the worse? The cold calculated killer approved by society, or the weak, sick man, deceived and trapped by evil?"

The judge began to sweat as the words continued, "And, if it were your children, wouldn't you be lenient?"

"Fifteen years imprisonment with the chance for parole, if he is a model prisoner," snapped out the judge, as he then banged his hammer down and rose to leave the court.

Before he left, he took another look at the prisoner and saw the man crying with relief and whispering, "Thank you, and God bless you," to him.

The prosecutor looked stunned as he stood there with the sentence going over and over in his mind. "Only fifteen years," he thought dejectedly. Then, after the judge left the courtroom, the prosecutor sat down with thoughts of anger on his mind, when all of a sudden he heard a voice in his head say, "Where has all the love and compassion you used to have gone? When you studied law, you did so to help people; how does killing them help?" The prosecutor shook his head saying to himself, "I am imagining it." He then rose and left for his office.

On the way to the office, he decided to stop for a drink and pulled into a bar where he had some whisky, after which he returned to his car continuing on to his office. As he drove along, all of a sudden a young boy ran out in front of him and the lawyer stepped hard on his brakes. The car stopped less than an inch from the young boy, whose mother ran screaming into the road and grabbed the boy.

"Thank God!" cried the mother. "Thank God you are all right." Then she looked into the car calling out, "You were speeding. This is a residential area; you should be more careful; you are a danger to society!"

The mother then left carrying her child with her. The lawyer pulled his car to the side of the road and slumped over the wheel, crying with relief. "If you had killed him...you were speeding and under the influence of a drug. What should your sentence be?" asked the voice in his head.

"You were breaking the law on two counts and you could have killed a child...what do you deserve?" The internal voice continued. The lawyer thought for awhile, then said to himself, "Yes, I was drugged. Yes, I was breaking the law. If I had killed that child, it would be, in a way, a type of murder."

"What sentence should you get then?" asked the voice in his head.

The lawyer was silent, then said out loud. "A lenient one, I hope." As he said it, an awareness came into his heart that if he would want this for himself, shouldn't he want it for others as well? At that moment he knew prosecution would no longer be his job, for now he wanted to defend people.

The voice in his head said, "Remember the Commandment, *Thou Shalt Not Kill*, and remember no matter what wrong a person may have done, this Commandment should not be broken, even in the name of justice, for this is the law of God, and it is the Law all are called to live by."

87.

8/27/99 — Jesus

EYES OF LOVE

As two men sat discussing their families, one said, "My wife is beautiful. I don't know how someone like me could have married such a woman. She had her choice of men, but she chose me. I can never understand it."

"It must be true love then," said the other. "You are a lucky man to have a wife like that...one who truly loves you."

"Yes, I am lucky, aren't I?" replied the man.

"How did you meet?" asked the other.

"At church. We met at a church meeting," answered the man.

"You go to church?" asked the other, with surprise in his voice.

"Yes, we go often. When I met my wife, I had just been to a prayer group, and afterwards, while coffee was served, I was introduced to her. It was funny, because while we were praying I noticed her and made one of my prayers a request to meet and talk to her. It was answered quickly," stated the man, as he smiled remembering the moment.

"You surprise me. I didn't think you were a church-going man; you never mentioned it before," said the other.

"I have always gone to church since my parents took me as a child. I enjoy it and I feel at peace there," replied the man.

"Didn't you ever see your wife there before that day?" asked the other.

"No, it was her first time to the prayer group, and I don't remember ever seeing her in church either, even though she went there," the man replied.

"Well, it was your lucky night then," stated the other.

"I think it was a blessed night. You know, later when I was speaking to my wife, when she was my fiancé, she told me that when she was at church she asked God to find her a good husband. She told me that several men had been attracted to her previously, but all of them only saw the outer beauty of her face and figure. If ever she tried to talk about God to them, they were really not interested, even though some would pretend to be.

"My wife said she was wondering if she would ever meet anyone who saw past her physical appearance to the person within, and anyone who had a spiritual longing to know God as she had. That day in church, when she asked God for help, after Mass a friend she knew invited her to come to the prayer group the next day. She had never been to a prayer group and did not know what they were like; she thought it might be full of fanatics. Anyway, she decided to go and that's where we met. I think our meeting was blessed by God, because He answered our prayers."

"Are you happy now?" asked the other.

"Yes, we are. We love each other dearly and thank God each day for our marriage. We hope to have children soon," said the man. "But I still find it hard to believe I could have such a beautiful wife."

"Do you think God would listen to me?" inquired the other.

"Why wouldn't He? God loves us all the same," answered the man.

"My parents say they don't think I will ever find a wife. My brother and sister keep telling me not to give up, but I don't seem to meet any-one," explained the other.

"Well, why don't you turn to God. He often answers prayers in an unexpected way. All He asks of people is that they try to love Him, love each other, and live a good life, doing their best to follow His Commandments. It's not as demanding as many people think, for once you start to live this way, you find a happiness within that makes you want to keep trying to live as God asks.

"Sometimes people think loving God is crazy or is like slavery, but I know it is not. Loving God brings true freedom and sanity into your life, for that is what it has done for me, my wife, and many others I know. I am sure if you turn to Him, God will do this for you, also," suggested the man.

"Will I have to pray all the time?" asked the other, uncertainly.

"No, of course not. Just try to pray a little each day to start with, and see where God leads you in that. You might also want to go and see a priest for some advice," offered the man.

"A priest!" exclaimed the other. "I don't know about that."

"Priests will not bite your head off. They want to help you, and they can give you better advice than I can on what you should do to get to know God better. Priests are a wonderful resource for people. It's sad that people often do not see that. I have some priests as friends, and they have helped me a lot."

"Maybe I will see a priest," mused the other. "Maybe I will."

"Mr. Jones, Doctor will see you now," called a nurse from the corridor where the two men were waiting.

"That's me," said the man. "Maybe I'll see you in church one day," he asked of the other, as he turned his wheelchair and rolled it down the corridor towards the waiting nurse.

"Yes, I think you might," said the other, as he sat there in his wheelchair, thinking about how God had helped the man, not only in his marriage but also in the peace he saw in the man's face... a peace he didn't often see in those who suffered, and a peace that he wanted.

He closed his eyes and said to himself, "God, help me."

This was the first time in his life he had asked God for help, and he felt a little unsure until he felt a hand touching his, and a gentle male voice, saying, "Are you all right; is there anything I can do to help?"

He opened his eyes to see a priest leaning over him and smiling, "I...uh," he stuttered.

"You looked like you needed help. I am Fr. Martin, the hospital chaplain. Can I help you?" asked the priest.

"I think you can, Father," said the man, as he smiled back at the priest, knowing God had heard him and sent him some help.

9/3/99 — God the Father

WILL I BE STRONG ENOUGH?

The older man sat back in his chair and let out a sigh, as he said, "Well, it's been a hard day. Two funerals, a wedding, a baptism, and a call to the hospital to administer the last rites; so much in one day, but that's the life of a priest!"

"Yes, but it is so rewarding," replied the young deacon, who would himself soon be a priest, for his ordination was only a couple of months away.

"Rewarding," said the older priest. "Of course it is. You know, every night, regardless of how tired I am, I give thanks to God for allowing me to be His servant. As I finish giving thanks, I never forget to ask for the strength of His Spirit to fill these tired old bones for the next day ahead. To me, that is my priesthood, doing God's Will by serving Him as a priest, thanking Him for all that happens in my life, and then asking Him to help me to carry on."

"Father, how long have you been ordained?" asked the deacon.

"Nearly 47 years now," smiled the old priest, contentedly.

"Did you ever doubt that you had made the right decision in becoming a priest?" inquired the deacon.

"Doubt? Of course I did. Sometimes when I was feeling a little lonely and I would see families... I wondered. Sometimes when people treated me badly or accused me of bad things...I wondered. Sometimes when I was exhausted...I wondered," answered the priest.

"How did you overcome these doubts...it must have been hard? You know I want to be a priest, but sometimes I wonder...will I be strong enough? I love God and I long to serve Him, but will I be able to do it?" asked the deacon, with a worried look on his face.

"Well, Son, you are no different from many who become priests. Most of those I know have wondered, just like you do and I have, yet they have made wonderful priests, fulfilling their sacred vows in every way. You know, when I felt the doubts creeping into my heart, I prayed in front of our Blessed Lord, and just spent time with Him. Again I asked...I asked for the grace of the Holy Spirit to overcome my human weaknesses and to be able to use them for the glory of God.

"Then, one day, I began to see the lonely feelings I had seen, at times, in the faces of others, those who had no one to love them. Now I began to understand them a little better, and as I reached out to them, I found, not only did it help them, but that it also helped me, as my loneliness was lifted. When I saw others being treated badly, I thought of how I felt when this happened to me, and all I wanted to do was comfort and support them.

"When I saw a poor family struggling to support themselves and exhausted from doing so, I knew some of what they were feeling, as I thought of my exhausted moments...so I would offer them help, and I would be there for them, encouraging them to carry on.

"So you see, the Holy Spirit showed me in my weaknesses how I can use them to relate to others and to help others. Doing so, the weaknesses became strengths, and I began to thank God for allowing me to have these moments of wondering, because with His help, I could grow through them, and I could help others in a way I had never known before," explained the old priest.

"I think that's why so many of your parishioners treat you as family," said the deacon.

"Well, we are family, aren't we? And how could I ever be lonely now with such a family around me?" smiled the old priest, as he thought of the many people in his parish that he had ministered to for years.

"I hope one day I will have a family like that," said the deacon.

"You will have, if you always remember you are here to serve God and serve His children. Remember, also, to thank Him for all things, and remember always to ask Him for the strength you need to fulfill your vows as a priest. Do this, and by the grace of God, you will make a wonderful priest," said the old priest assuredly, as he closed his eyes and said in his mind, "Thank You, Lord, for my priesthood. Thank You, Lord, for today, and Lord, please give me the strength to serve You in another day."

The next moment he was snoring heavily as he fell asleep in the chair. The young deacon went and got a blanket and laid it over the sleeping priest and said, quietly, "Oh Lord, help me to be a good priest like Father here, and Lord give me the strength to never stop thanking You, whatever may come my way."

The deacon went to his room with a confidence in his heart that whatever happened in the future, God would give him the strength he needed, that through the deacon's humanity, God would grant him the graces to be a good priest.

10/3/99 — Jesus

HE CALLED HER MOTHER

The nurse called out, "Doctor, come quickly, I think he is going!"

The doctor came rushing into the room with his white gown flapping behind him.

"Let me see," he said, as he leaned over the man lying in the bed, while looking into his eyes and placing a stethoscope on his chest to listen to his heart.

"I don't think there is much we can do now; it is in God's hands," said the doctor, sadly.

"Surely you should try something?" questioned the nurse, with surprise in her voice.

"He is riddled with cancer; it is throughout his body. We have not been able to do anything for him except ease his pain. Unfortunately, there is nothing more we can do; it is his time to go, I think," replied the doctor, as he gently stroked the hair of the dying man before him.

"It seems such a waste. He is so young and so good-looking," stated the nurse.

"Yes, he is young and it is sad, but if he dies, at least his suffering will be over," replied the doctor, gently.

Just then the man in the bed opened his eyes and looked at the doctor above him, then smiled weakly, as he whispered, "Doctor, please tell my wife I was thinking of her, and that I will love her for eternity."

"I will, I promise," replied the doctor, smiling back at the man.

"Thank you," whispered the man, as he closed his eyes and took his last breath.

The doctor examined the man and confirmed he was dead, then asked the nurse to make the necessary arrangements. The nurse nodded silently, and the doctor could see a little tear rolling down her cheek.

"It's not the end, you know," said the doctor. "He has gone to a better place, where I am sure he will be happy in the arms of God."

The nurse looked at him, and said, "I hope so; he suffered a lot here."

At that moment, another nurse came into the room, saying, "His wife is here. Will I send her in?"

"No, I will come and speak to her first," replied the doctor, as he made his way to the reception area.

"Doctor, how is he?" asked the wife, as she saw the doctor approaching.

"Maybe we can speak in here," suggested the doctor, opening the door to a side room.

The wife stared at him with a solemn face. "He's not dead yet, is he Doctor?" she asked.

"Come in here, where we can talk privately," beckoned the doctor.

"Oh, no!" wailed the wife, as tears welled in her eyes. "Please don't tell me he's dead. Please, please," she begged, as the doctor took her hand to lead her into the room. Then, as the realization of her husband's death came upon her, she called out, "He is...he's dead!" As she said this, her legs gave way underneath her and she fell to the floor, sobbing. The doctor reached down and gently lifted her up, then held her close to him, as the wife cried on his shoulder.

Two nurses came to help, and with the doctor, took the woman into the room and placed her in a soft chair.

"It was a peaceful death...just a few minutes ago. Before he died he told me to tell you he would love you in eternity. Those were his last words; words for you."

"Can I see him now?" sobbed the woman.

"In a little while; just take a moment to recover," suggested the doctor.

"I am all right. I have been expecting this for a long time, but now it has happened..." sobbed the woman.

"He did see a priest before he died and received the Last Rites. I think the priest is still here, if you would like to speak to him," asked the doctor.

"Yes...yes, I would, but can I see my husband first?" implored the woman.

"Yes, of course," replied the doctor. "Come with me." Together they walked in silence to the room. "Shall I leave you alone for a while?" asked the doctor.

"Yes, please," replied the woman, quietly.

When the doctor had gone, she went nervously to the bed where her husband lay.

"You look at peace, my love," she sobbed, as she fell on her husband, embracing and kissing his still body.

"At least you are out of pain now, my darling," sobbed the woman putting her cheek against her husband's. With her hand, she reached along his arm to place her hand in his. As she came to his hand, she found it was closed, holding tightly onto his Rosary. The woman smiled, and said, gently, "I know Mother Mary is taking care of you. Let's say a Rosary together now for the last time."

The wife began to pray the Rosary half expecting to hear her husband join in, but there was nothing. A few minutes later she heard the door to the room open and someone walk in, but she did not care, she lay there with her husband praying the Rosary. Then she heard the voice she knew to be the priest, joining in with her prayers. All of a sudden she felt a peace enter her body, and she knew everything would be all right; she knew her husband was happy.

"My dear, are you all right?" asked the priest, as he came and placed his hand on her shoulder.

"Yes, Father, I am," replied the still crying, but now smiling woman.

"I know he is with God, and that Mother Mary is caring for him, and I know he is still loving me."

"My dear, I spoke to him just a little while ago, and I brought him Communion and heard his confession. I believe he went to face God with a clean heart, and his soul united in Jesus. I am sure he will be given eternal peace by God," explained the priest.

"Thank you, Father, thank you," said the wife as she rose from the bed, stroking her husband's face, as she did.

"Shall we have a cup of tea?" suggested the priest.

"No, Father, if it is all right with you. I would like just to sit here for a little while with my husband," answered the woman.

"Of course. Would you like me to stay with you?" asked the priest.

"Yes, please, Father," responded the wife, and so together they sat there silently in prayer and in their thoughts. The nurse, who had been with the man when he died entered the room, unaware the two were in there.

"Oh, sorry. I didn't know you were here. Shall I come back later?" she asked. The priest nodded gently at her, and the nurse began to leave the room.

"Were you with him when he died?" asked the wife.

"Yes, I was, and it was very peaceful. His last words were of you," explained the nurse, gently.

"Thank you," said the wife, as she went back to her thoughts.

Just then, the Rosary the dead man had been holding fell to the ground.

"How did that get back in his hand? I took it out once already. Maybe his mother put it back in his hand," said the nurse, as she bent down to pick up the Rosary beads.

"His mother?" asked the wife.

"Yes, she was here a few minutes ago. I thought she would still be here when you came, but she must have gone," said the nurse.

"She had put these in his hand before he died and was back later after he died. I think she must have put them back in his hand then."

"His mother has lived overseas for a long time. She doesn't even know he is...he was ill," said the wife, not sure who had visited her husband.

"Well, she said she was his mother, and when he first saw her, he was smiling and tried to sit up to greet her, but he didn't have the strength. He called her mother," stated the nurse, worried in case she had made a mistake.

"What did she look like?" asked the priest.

"Well, she was dressed in blue; she had a beautiful face, so gentle and warm. You could tell she loved him, for she held his head in her arms like a baby; it was very moving. I heard her say to him that his Father was waiting for him. It was then he smiled, closed his eyes, and I knew he was dying, so I called the doctor.

When he came, the mother had gone. She must have moved quickly, for I didn't see her leave. Then, after the doctor went to meet you, she came back again. I'll look for her if you like," suggested the nurse.

"No, it will be all right," said the wife, smiling broadly. "His Mother Mary was here."

The priest sat silently, amazed at what he had just heard.

"I'll come back later, then," said the nurse, as she left the room, wondering why a wife would be smiling like that when her husband had just died. Back in the room, the woman sat smiling, rocking back and forth, saying over and over, "His Mother Mary was here," while the priest got on his knees praying and thanking God for His merciful Mother.

<u>10/25/99 — *Jesus*</u>

SHE KNOWS ME!

"But, surely, it is their own fault that they are poor!" exclaimed the wealthy man, as he looked out of the window from the train he was on, which was traveling at high speed through a very poor area.

"No, dear; it is not," replied his wife. "These people have not had the opportunity that we have had. That is the main reason for their poverty."

"Most of them are lazy!" snapped the husband. "Even when they are given jobs, they are either incapable of doing them, or just cannot be bothered to do the work properly."

"Well, if they are incapable, that is because they have not had the opportunity to be educated in the skills they need to do the work. Surely, time should be given to help them achieve those abilities," suggested the wife.

"Huh!" snorted the husband. "Anyway, most of them do not want to work; they are happier lazing around all day."

"But dear, I see many of them who do get jobs, working very hard and long hours," stated the wife. "And they seem so happy that there is work for them to earn a wage."

"Yes, but what do they do with the money? These slums never change. No matter how many of these people work, the slums will stay, because this is how the people who live here like it!" retorted the husband.

"I think it probably has more to do with the low wages that are paid. Maybe by the time food and clothing have been bought, there is no money left for anything else," said the wife.

"Well, we can't pay them any more. That's how we keep our prices down and make the profits, so you and I can live as we do," smiled the husband, condescendingly.

The wife looked at her husband, then looked out of the window into the slum-city. As the train sped along, she could see, time and again, poor people who looked so cold, so hungry, and so in need of help.

"So, we should ignore them, then?" she asked.

"Everyone else does," replied the husband, as he picked up a paper and began to read it.

"Well, I can't," said the wife, firmly.

The husband lowered the paper and looked at his wife. "What do you think you can do?" he almost laughed, as he said the words.

"First, I want you to increase the wages of our workers so they can live better," replied the wife.

"What! You have got to be joking...that would cut our profits," said the husband in disbelief.

"Well, we would still make profits, wouldn't we?" asked the wife.

"Yes, but a lot less than now," answered the husband.

"But we have lots of money in the bank, enough to live a good life until we die, and much, much more," stated the wife.

"Yes, that's true, but that doesn't mean we should give away our profits from our investment and hard work," said the husband, with disbelief in his voice.

"Why not?" asked the wife, as she continued. "Surely, if we have more than enough, it is only greed that makes us seek more. If others are living in poverty working for us, and we make profits from their work, surely then that is wrong; surely it is a sin!" The husband said nothing as his wife carried on.

"If they work hard and barely survive, yet we profit from that, it must be wrong. It is our duty as Christians not to profit from the suffering of others. We must pay them more. Don't you see that, darling?" asked the wife, smiling at her husband.

The man sat there thinking of the lower profits his company would make, and how he did not like to lose his profit margin when it was unnecessary to do so.

"And think, my husband, one day in the not too distant future, this life will be over and money will mean nothing then. When you face God and He asks why you had so much and did so little to help the poor, what will you say? I wonder also what reward God will give to you...Heaven or Hell. It is how you live in this life that has bearing upon that. I think we should take the opportunity now to change our lives and start helping the needy, as God would expect us to do," suggested the wife.

As the husband listened to her words, he knew what she said was true, but he tried to push it aside. Just then a nun came into the compartment and sat down looking out of the window.

"How sad," she whispered, quietly. The man looked at the nun and saw a beauty in her face that seemed to shine from it, but also a deep sadness.

"We were just talking about the slums," said the wife to the nun.

"That's where I work," smiled the nun.

"It must be hard for you," inquired the wife.

"Yes, it is," said the nun. "Always the sick, the hungry, and the poor, and never enough food, medicine, or money. I pray that more wealthy Christians would live as Jesus asked them to and give to the poor, instead of being blind to them, and often even accusing the poor of bringing everything upon themselves."

The husband felt these words touch his heart and his face reddened, as he knew deep inside this nun was speaking about him...but how did she know what they had been discussing?

The nun looked at the man and, smiling said, "Are you all right? You look a little flushed."

"I...I...I'm all right...thank you," stuttered the man.

"Maybe we can help your mission in some way," asked the wife.

"That's kind of you," said the nun.

"What can we do?" asked the wife again of the nun.

"Well, money for food and medicine would help, or even if it were possible, money to build a clean surgery for our voluntary doctors," replied the nun.

"Doesn't the government supply the doctors and a surgery?" cut in the husband.

"No, just like everyone else, the poor are expected to pay. You know, even when people from among the poor find work, their wages are so low that they are not much better off, and so even the workers cannot afford medicine and doctors. What a shame it is that many employers take advantage of the poor and perpetuate their poverty by paying them low wages," said the nun, as she stared directly at the man.

The wife looked at her husband who was still red in the face. "Yes, it is a shame, a shame of mankind," she said, gently.

The man's heart was racing as he thought, "She knows me; how is that possible?"

The nun continued, "You know, it is never too late to make amends in one's life for ignoring, mistreating, or taking advantage of the poor, and I pray many of the well-to-do remember that. Jesus said, 'You will always have the poor with you,' so that means people always have the opportunity to help the poor, and in doing so, help themselves grow in the grace and the love of God. I pray the wealthy stop seeing the poor as a burden, and start to see them as a grace-filled way of coming closer to God and the eternal reward of Heaven."

As the nun said the last word, it echoed in the wealthy man's heart, and he knew at that moment, if he did nothing to help the poor, that he was risking losing Heaven.

Sweat ran down his face, as he said, very quickly, to the nun, "We were just talking about that, and I was going to do something to help those poor people."

Reaching into his pocket he pulled out his checkbook and began to write. At first he was only going to give a token offering, when inside he thought he heard a voice say, "If you are not generous, can you expect God to be generous to you?"

At that moment the nun spoke, saying, "God is generous to the generous of heart."

The man began to shake a little and then, in his mind, he saw many of the beggars who had asked for money from him, but from whom he had turned away. He saw many of the sick and suffering that he had walked past, ignoring them, and then he saw Jesus suffering on the Cross, and he was turning and walking away from Jesus.

He wanted to cry, as now it dawned on him how he had been rejecting God's call to him in his life: the call to love and help others. Now the man felt terrible within, and he found it hard to control his shaking and to not cry.

The man looked at his checkbook in his hand, ripped out the check he had half written and tore it up. Then, remembering what wealth he had, the man wrote a substantial amount on the check and handed it to the nun.

"Why, thank you," said the nun with a smile. "You are so generous. This will build a clean surgery and buy a lot of medicine. Thank you, and God bless you."

The wife smiled gently at her husband, as if to say, "Well done!"

"And I am going to increase the wages of my workers from today," said the man. "I didn't really think about them before, but today, you, Sister, and my wife, have made me think."

"Thank you, dear," said the wife, happily.

"Sadly, many of the wealthy do not think of the poor today. I thank God that in some way I have helped you to do so," stated the nun, with a truly thankful look on her face.

"Dear wife, you said firstly you would like to see wages increased. What was the second thing?" asked the husband of the wife.

"That you give to the poor, and you have done that," said the wife, smiling contentedly. "I was also praying for one other thing," she said.

"What was it dear?" asked the husband, who was now feeling a peace in his heart he had never known before.

"That through the poor, you would come to find Jesus and His peace," replied the hopeful sounding wife.

"Well, your prayer has been answered, for I surely have," stated the man, as he looked lovingly at this wife.

"Thank God," cried the wife, as she knew from the look on his face that her husband spoke the truth.

"Yes, thank God," added the nun. "For I was praying that today God would bring what was needed for my work with the poor. I also prayed that in doing so, a soul would be touched by God's love and mercy to know God's expectations and God's generosity. How good is God!"

Together the three of them sat there discussing what had just happened among them, and planning what they could do together in the future to help the poor. Religious and laity working together in God's love, the way God planned it, the way it was meant to be.

WHEN YOU CAME TO HER

As the priest raised his hands that held the bread and wine of Communion, he wondered, "Is this really the Body and Blood of Jesus?" He tried to push this thought from his mind, and continued with the Mass.

When Mass was over and all the people had left the Church, the priest sat quietly alone before the altar. In his mind the priest was going over and over all he had learned about the Eucharist in the seminary many years ago. He also remembered passages and quotations from the many books he had read on the Eucharist. He thought about the many Eucharistic miracles that had happened throughout the history of the Church, and of the many personal testimonies on the power of the Eucharist that he had heard.

"Why, oh why, Lord, do these doubts still plague me?" he asked aloud, and sat silently hoping for an answer or a divine revelation. He heard or saw nothing. Yet he remained there, and began to pray in his mind.

The next thing the priest knew, was waking suddenly from the sleep he had fallen into. The priest rubbed his eyes and then noticed a young boy kneeling at the front of the altar praying out loud.

"Jesus," said the boy, "I know You are here, and I know You are listening to me. Well, Jesus, I just came to say thank You for looking after my mother. Jesus, do You remember I asked You last week not to let my mother die, and to save my baby brother inside of her? Well, thank You for helping. I know You did. Mother was dying, but when You came to her, she was all right and so

was my baby brother. Thank You Jesus, I promise
I will try to be good every day from now on.
Amen."

The boy stood up and began to leave the Church,
when the priest called out, "Son, come here a
minute please."

"Yes, Father," replied the boy, who then came
shyly over to the priest.

"I didn't mean any harm, Father. I was just
speaking to Jesus," said the boy, who was about
ten years old.

"That's all right, son; don't I know you?" asked
the priest.

"Yes, Father, we come here to Mass on Sundays,
but usually the other priest says that Mass,"
answered the boy.

"Oh, you mean Father Michael," said the priest,
and the boy nodded in agreement.

"Son, can I ask you something?" inquired the
priest.

The boy replied, "Yes."

"You said Jesus came to your mother; when was
that?" asked the priest.

"My Mother is in hospital with my baby brother
but the doctors had told my Dad she would
probably die unless my baby brother was killed.
Well, Mum and Dad wouldn't let them kill my
brother, and said they would trust in God. Mum
and Dad said Jesus would take care of them, and
He did," said the smiling boy.

"How?" asked the priest.

"Jesus came to her in the hospital, and everything was all right," stated the boy.

"Jesus came to her!" exclaimed the priest.

"Of course," said the boy, surprised that the
priest did not know that.

"How?" asked the priest.

"Father Michael brought Him, and my mother
had Communion before her operation. Then every-

thing was all right," said the boy, matter-of-factly.

"Is that so?" said the priest.

"Yes, and my mum told me, that from the moment she had Communion until she woke with my baby brother in her arms, she could see Jesus' face. So you see, He was there," said the boy.

"Yes, it seems He was," smiled the priest.

"And I am going to pray a thank You to Jesus every day from now on," said the boy.

"Good boy," replied the priest as he reached into his pocket and pulled out his Rosary. Handing it to the boy, he said, "Here, use this in the future."

The boy took it, smiled, and said, "Thank you, Father, for your gift. I had better go home now," and then the boy left, Rosary in hand.

The priest looked up at the Tabernacle and said, "And thank You, Jesus, for Your gift to me."

In the priest's heart now, there was no doubt and no fear of the uncertainties he had at times, for now Jesus had shown him clearly the truth. The truth that Jesus is the Eucharist, and in the Eucharist, Jesus is with His people, and His people are with Him. The truth the priest would never doubt again.

11/5/99 — God the Father

STOP WORRYING!

"The world seems so bad today!" stated the man to his friend, as they left the church. "I am sure God will not put up with this much longer. There seems to be sin everywhere you look."

"Ah...yes, but there is a lot of good happening, also," replied the friend.

"Well, I don't see much of that," responded the man.

"What about all the people who go to Church? What about many of the young people today who are turning to God? What about the people who help when disasters strike? What about the people who give to help the poor? What about the people who stand for peace? What about the people who stand against sin? What about the people who try to bring a better life for all people on earth? If you add these people, and the many more who try to do what is right in their lives, you would find there is a lot of good in the world," suggested the friend.

"All I ever see is bad happening: wars, disasters, starvation, people not interested in God, greed, selfishness, free sex, drugs, violence, lots of crime, lots of anger, and hatred. The world today is a bad place!" stated the man.

"Well, if you look for these things, you will find them, for they are happening, but if you look for good, you will find that, too, for it is there; it is just how you look," replied the friend.

"I'm sure God will not put up with this much longer," said the man, as he shook his head in disgust.

"God is merciful; it says so in Holy Scripture, and we humans can never understand His mercy. I think, however, as long as there are people living for Him in the world, trying to live according to His Commandments, sacrificing for His love, and praying for others, then I think God will continue to shower His merciful love upon mankind, giving people every opportunity to change their lives and come to Him. If this were not so, I think God would have destroyed mankind long before now," stated the friend.

"When?" snapped the man. "The world has never been so bad!"

"Is that really so?" inquired the friend. "Think about fascism and communism's time; think how sin flourished then. Millions killed, many more suffering; force was used in an effort to stop people from loving God. Terrible, terrible things happened, but often they were hidden from view. Much of what happens today happened then, but it was hidden from the public. How many children were killed? Women raped? People tortured and murdered? People enslaved? Freedom was denied for so many; how can you say it is worse today? I think the only difference is that we see it more clearly today."

"Maybe you are right," mused the man. "There was a lot of sin then. I suppose people at that time wondered why God didn't come and destroy mankind."

"I think God is so merciful that He will give mankind as much time as is necessary, and I don't think we as humans will be able to guess what the Divine Will is. I think we should just keep loving God, serving Him, reaching out to others in love, and trusting that God will continue to be merciful to mankind," suggested the friend, with a smile. "For I think that is how God wants us to be."

"You know, I think you are right," replied the man. "Why worry? Leave it to God."

"Well, that's what Jesus showed in Holy Scripture. His life was not one of worry, but one of complete trust in the Father, knowing the Father's Will was and is the same as His will: merciful and forgiving. If we as Christians are to follow Christ our Lord, we should follow Him in trust, as He showed us in His life," explained the friend.

"From today," said the man, "I am going to stop worrying about all the bad and focus on the good, trusting that in God's Will, the good will grow in the world and many will be saved in His mercy."

"Stop worrying, but don't stop praying and working for good to grow, because God wants not only your trust, but your action also," responded the friend.

The man smiled at his friend, and said, "Thank you for reminding me what loving God means: to trust Him, to work for Him and to help others do the same, and to have no fear in your life, only security in Him."

Together, the two walked off discussing how they should pray more for the salvation of souls, and how they could encourage others to join them in this, and the works they were planning, to help spread the goodness of God in the future.

11/7/99 — Jesus

PRECIOUS GIFTS

"I don't want it," cried the woman. "I am too young to have a baby. It will spoil my life. I've got so much I want to do before I have children. The time is not right; it doesn't suit me. I will get rid of it!"

"But it's a baby...our baby!" pleaded her husband.

"I don't care. I don't want to be tied down by a child!" snapped the woman.

"But our baby is alive inside of you...our son or our daughter," replied the husband, gently.

"I bet it would be a different story if you were pregnant," moaned the wife.

"Come on; just think about what you are saying," suggested the husband. "You have our baby, our child within you. It's not the end of the world, but it can be the beginning of a happy family. You can still do the things you want to. Yes, there will be some limitations because of the baby, but together we can overcome them."

"I want an abortion. Lots of people have them. It's only a small procedure," stated the wife.

"You would kill our baby?" asked the husband in disbelief.

"It's not a baby yet. It's only a fertilized egg. It doesn't become a baby for weeks," replied the wife, matter-of-factly.

"That's not true," said the husband. "From the moment of conception, it is a baby...our baby."

"The doctors think differently. Many of them say it is not a baby for weeks, as it has no arms, no legs, no brain, and no heart. Nothing really. That's what it is...a nothing," said the woman, with a certainty in her voice.

"You know that's not true. Life is there. God-given life, and it is wrong to deny it, to kill it," explained the husband.

"Well, God would have known I didn't want a baby yet, so why would He give me one? Tell me that!" retorted the wife.

"Obviously God thinks it is the right time. I mean we are married. We love each other. We want a family, don't we?" asked the husband.

"Yes...yes, but not now," answered the wife. "It's the wrong time."

"How can it be? You are pregnant. You have our baby within you...our child conceived in the love we have for each other."

As he said this, the husband put his arm around his wife and continued, "I love you and I love our baby within you. Together we can bring our child up, and together we can make it possible to still enjoy life."

"No...no. I don't want it!" shouted the wife, as she broke free from his embrace.

"I thought this marriage was 'us.' All I seem to hear is what you want. What about me?" asked the husband, quietly.

"I love you," replied the wife. "You are my husband."

"If you love me, why do you want to kill my child?" quizzed the husband.

"It's not killing your child. I will just be getting rid of a fertilized egg. That's all," said the wife, with a note of justification in her voice.

"That fertilized egg, as you call it, is fertilized by me and it is your egg. Now it has the spark of life that God has placed in it, so it is your egg and my sperm, joined in the gift of life from God. It is alive.

If allowed to, it will grow and grow to become our baby, then a child, a teenager, an adult and one day, our baby may bring us grandchildren. Inside you now is part of the future of our family, part of the future of the world, and you want to destroy that. Can't you see it's wrong, not only for the life you would deny now, but for the effect on the future of that God-given life being denied? This is our child. Don't kill our baby, please, my love," said the husband, in a pleading voice.

"You don't seem to hear what I am saying. Do I have to spell it out to you? I DON'T WANT THIS BABY!" shouted the wife; "It's my right not to have it."

"What about my rights and the rights of our baby within you?" asked the husband.

"You don't have any. It's my body and I will do what I want with it," retorted the wife.

"What has happened to the woman I knew and loved?" asked the husband, as he shook his head from side to side.

"I am still here, but I have my rights!" snapped the wife.

"I don't think she is here anymore, for the woman I knew loved little babies, and always smiled at them," recollected the husband.

"This is not a baby yet. Don't you understand?" said the wife.

"I think maybe it is you who does not understand. You have a living being within you. If this were not so, if you did nothing to the egg, it would develop into a child. It is alive and it is a baby, and if left alone, it will grow into a complete human being. That in itself proves it is alive," reasoned the husband.

The wife sat quietly and said nothing. "I think the only thing that does not have life in it is your heart," said the frustrated and disappointed husband.

The wife leaned forward and switched on the television to avoid further conversation with her husband.

As the television came to life, the news program was showing a story about a woman who had lost her two children in an accident recently, but had just discovered she was pregnant again.

"You must be happy to be pregnant again after the loss of your other children," suggested the news reporter.

"Yes, I am," smiled the pregnant woman in reply. "And I thank God for this wonderful gift. After losing my babies, I never thought I would have any more, because I am a little old. I pray nothing happens to this one."

"How many months is it now?" inquired the reporter.

"The pregnancy...two months. Since I lost my children...six months," replied the pregnant woman.

The wife, sitting on the chair said, softly, "I am two months."

"Are you hoping for a girl or boy?" asked the reporter.

"I don't care. I just pray my baby is healthy. I keep thinking about how good God has been to me, giving me this unexpected chance to bring a life into the world. I think this is one of the most wonderful things a woman can do; bring God's gift of life into the world. I can never understand women who do not want their babies.

"You know, the children I lost were only with me a few years, but I would not have missed those years for anything...the love we shared, the happiness...so many wonderful experiences that will be with me always. How could anyone ever want to miss those times? The lives of children are so precious, and I thank God from my heart for the chance of another one," responded the pregnant woman.

"And the children brought us closer together, gave us a deeper love," said the pregnant woman's husband as he put his arm around his wife, who was being interviewed.

Then finishing on that scene, the news moved on to another story. The woman watching the television sat quietly for a time and then turned to her husband, saying, "Even after all her pain, that woman is happy being pregnant. Why aren't I?"

"Maybe it was the fact that the woman saw the lives given through her and her husband were precious gifts of God's love. Did you hear how she kept thanking God for her children and her time with them? Did you see how happy she was? Well, it looked like that happiness was found in her family, in her husband and her children, even though they died. That's a happiness that only comes in family and in God," replied the husband.

"Yes, she had a peace, didn't she?" mused the wife.

"I don't think any of my friends have that peace. Even though my friends lead busy and exciting lives, my friends don't seem to have that happiness, either."

"Well, your friends don't have children, do they? Most of your friends have had abortions; no wonder they don't have the peace and happiness that woman and her husband have, even through tragedy," suggested the husband.

"Her husband said the children deepened their love," stated the wife.

"Yes, children can do that, for children that are loved bring love into many families," said the husband.

"It must be a lot of work to look after two children, like she did," commented the wife.

"Well, in a family both husband and wife have the responsibility to share the load," replied the husband. "The sharing," he continued, "is a sign of love for each other and for the children. I think that is why the woman's husband on the news said their love deepened."

The wife went and sat next to her husband and snuggled against him.

"I'm sorry," she said. "I was worried. I have never been pregnant before, and I didn't want to lose all the good things we have now and the freedom to do as we want. After seeing that couple on the news, those things don't seem so important now. They looked happier than I thought possible, especially after losing two children. You know, every time she mentioned God and what a gift from Him children are, I got a sensation in my womb, a burning. I think she is right. I have a feeling inside that what she said is the truth. Darling, I don't want an abortion anymore; it all of a sudden seems so wrong. How could I hurt our baby? How could I hurt you? And, how could I ever think that way?"

"You were a little confused my dear. It's all right; everything will be okay from now on; wait and see," smiled the husband, as he kissed his wife, lovingly.

"We are going to have a baby!" said the wife, happily.

"Yes, we are. Thank God for that, and thank God for the love He has given to us," suggested the husband.

"There is a lot to thank Him for," said the wife, placing her hand and his on her stomach.

The sensation was there again and she knew deep in her heart that this was God giving her a sign: she had made the right decision and all would be well from now on.

11/9/99 — Jesus

MY FRIEND LOVED ME

"I wonder how I can go on. Nothing seems to go right in my life. Everything I touch seems to fall apart. Everything I try to do fails!" said a dejected young man to his friend.

"I see everyone else doing okay; they have jobs, money, cars, clothes, friends. What have I got? Nothing! You're my only friend; I don't know what I would do without you. Why is life so hard?"

His friend looked at him with big brown eyes and leaned over to lick his face.

"Good boy. You love me, don't you?" said the young man as he ruffled the hair of the dog. "And you never complain about me, do you boy?"

The dog wagged his tail contentedly, but feeling the sadness of his owner, licked him again and then leaned against the young man with almost his whole body weight.

"I wonder how it got so bad," said the man to his dog. "I used to have friends. I had a job. I had money. I had it all. Now it's all gone and all I have is you and my habit."

The dog let out a little whine, as he sat leaning on his owner.

"This habit..." said the young man, as he stretched out his right arm to look at the needle marks, "...this habit has destroyed my life. It's taken everything away from me." The young man sat quietly and looked up at the stars in the night sky.

"Oh God," he called out loud, "how did I ever get this way?"

He waited almost expecting an answer, but the night air was still. "I hope, my friend, someone will take care of you when I'm gone," he said to his dog. Again, sensing something was wrong, the dog whined and then once more licked the young man's face.

The man smiled at the dog, saying, "You will be all right, you will find your way home to Mom and Dad."

As he finished saying that, he thought of his parents and of the many arguments they had since he started taking drugs. He remembered it was never like that before the drugs. He thought of how he stole from his parents, his brothers, his sister, and his friends. He thought of the times he stole from strangers, and how recently he had sold his body to another man so he could get money for drugs. Tears welled in his eyes as he cried out loud, "Oh God, how did I fall so far? If You're out there God, forgive me for the pain I've caused. Oh God, I can't see any way out of this; it's only getting worse."

Now the young man was sobbing as he blurted out the words, "God, please forgive me, and forgive me for what I'm about to do, but I can't go on anymore."

Now the dog was whimpering as he saw in his owner's hand a large knife. The dog was almost pleading with the young man, for he sensed the danger.

"My friend, I won't hurt you, and I won't hurt anyone ever again. This is my only way out," said the young man in a nervous voice. Then he pushed the dog away as he raised the knife, preparing to plunge it into his heart. "God forgive me," he cried as he closed his eyes and brought the knife down towards his chest. He heard a whine as he felt the knife enter flesh but realized it wasn't his flesh. He opened his eyes to see his dog between him and the knife, with the knife embedded deep in the dog's stomach. "Oh no! Oh no!" he cried out loud as the dog's blood began to run onto his hand.

"I'm sorry, I'm sorry," he sobbed, as he held his dog. The dying dog looked up at his master and struggled to turn his head, weakly lifting it to be able to lick his master's face one more time, then the dog's head fell sideways as he died. "What have I done?" cried the young man. Then at the top of his voice he shouted in a voice filled with the sorrow on his heart, "NO! NO!"

"What's wrong?" asked the priest who, with the nun he was accompanying from a Church meeting, had heard the young man's cries and had come to see what was wrong.

"I've killed my dog," sobbed the young man holding tightly onto the still warm body.

"How did it happen?" asked the nun, as she came and sat next to the man and put her arm around him.

"I killed him, and he was my only friend," sobbed the man. The priest leaned down and stroked the dead dog, asking, "Would you like me to bury him for you?"

"Huh...no, I will do it," answered the still sobbing man.

"There is a knife in him," stated the nun, as she noticed what was in the man's hand.

"How did it happen, Son?" inquired the priest.

"I was going to kill myself, and I closed my eyes as I built up the courage to stab myself, but my dog...my dog came between me and the knife," explained the young man with a voice full of emotion.

"Your dog must have loved you," said the priest.

"Yes, he did," replied the man.

"He loved you so much he gave his life to stop you killing yourself," said the nun, as she gently took the young man's hand off the knife.

There was silence for a moment, then the priest said, "You see, your dog knew that your life was precious, so he sacrificed his life for you. He obviously loved you."

"Yes, he was my only friend. I loved him and I've killed him," spluttered the young man. "I can't even do this right."

"Here, let me help you with the dog. We should take him and bury him. Where do you live?" asked the priest, as he gently lifted the dog from the man's lap.

"I live on the streets. I haven't got a home," replied the man.

"Well, where shall we bury him?" asked the priest. The young man just shrugged his shoulders saying, "I don't know."

"The convent is not far from here. Let's take the dog there. I am sure we can find a little space in the grounds for him," suggested the nun, as she held the arm of the still distraught young man.

As they stepped into the light, she saw the marks on his arm from the needles. "Why did you want to kill yourself?" asked the nun.

"I've got no future, nothing to look forward to, and when I look back, I only see pain," responded the young man. "There was...is nothing to live for. The only one who cared for me was my dog, and now he's gone."

"There is always Someone Who loves you, Who cares for you," said the nun.

"Who?" asked the man.

"God cares for you and loves you," replied the nun.

"God, I think, doesn't care for me anymore. I've done so many bad things, I doubt if He could ever forgive me," stated the man.

"God loves everyone, Son," said the priest. "And God is prepared to forgive any sin, if the person really wants forgiveness and tries to live a good life, once forgiven."

"How could God love me? I've hurt so many people. I've committed so many sins; I even disgust myself," replied the young man.

"Well, God showed His love of you tonight," suggested the priest.

"What do you mean?" asked the now confused man.

"Well, God created your dog in His love, and in God's love your dog loved you. When your dog saw that you were in danger, the love he had for you, the God-given love, made him want to save you, and so he sacrificed his life for you.

"In that sacrifice, your dog showed that God's love within him wanted to stop you from harming yourself. In this way, God is saying to you that your life is valuable, that you are loved and cared for, and that you should try again in life and not give up."

The young man looked at the priest and said, "I don't quite understand what you are saying, but I know it sounds right. Maybe God does love me. I know He created my friend," he stroked the body of the dog as he said this, "and my friend loved me."

"Don't you think you owe it to your dog to try to get your life together?" asked the nun, softly.

"Yes, I think I do," replied the man as he felt a strength inside him he had not known for a long while. "But how?" he asked.

"We will help you," suggested the nun.

"Will you really? I am a drug addict, but I do not want to be one anymore. Tonight, for the first time, I think I may be able to overcome my addiction," explained the young man.

"We know you are addicted to drugs and so does God, but that doesn't stop Him or us from loving you, and it doesn't stop us from wanting to help you," confirmed the priest.

"And if you are successful, your dog's sacrifice will not have been wasted," added the nun.

"No, it won't, will it?" exclaimed the young man.

"Come on, the convent's not far," encouraged the priest. "And after we've buried your friend, you can come and stay with me tonight."

"Thank you, Father," smiled the young man with the first smile he had in months.

"What was your dog's name?" asked the nun.

"Francis," answered the man, as he took the dog from the priest and began to carry him in the direction of the convent.

"And what order do you belong to, Sister?" inquired the man.

"Both Father and myself are Franciscans," responded the nun, gently.

Then the three walked on with the faithful dog. Unknown and unseen there was an Italian man, in a brown habit and sandals who walked beside them praying in thanks to God that once more, through an animal, God's love had been seen.

12/15/99 — God the Father

AM I NOTHING TO YOU, MUMMY?

The child felt comfortable and warm, feeling his mother surrounding him, feeling and sharing each heartbeat with his mother. Secure and at peace, the child awaited his coming life in the outside world.

"I think we should get rid of him," suggested the man to the woman he had made pregnant.

"But why?" asked the woman.

"Well, I am not going to marry you, and you will be by yourself with a child to take care of," he replied. "Anyway, you should have taken precautions; you should have been on the pill."

The woman looked at the man in disbelief. "Me?" she shrieked, "What about you? You are just as much to blame," she said, accusingly.

"Let's not argue over this, the best thing for all concerned is that you have an abortion, then there won't be a problem anymore."

The child inside the woman felt a coldness now touching him as each word the child's parents were saying reverberated around him. The previous feelings of warmth, security, and peace were vanishing fast, as the cold enveloped the child, who now, for the first time in his young life, was feeling a touch of evil. Fear filled the child as the words got louder and more bitter.

"This thing within me is yours!" screamed the woman. "Don't you have any feelings for him?"

"No, he means nothing to me. It's just an accident that happened one night," replied the man with no caring in his voice.

"If I get rid of him, I never want to see you again!" snapped the woman, bitterly.

"Suits me," said the man, nonchalantly.

"Will you pay for the abortion?" asked the woman.

"Yeah, I suppose I should," said the man, with relief in his voice, as he knew the woman was going to do as he asked.

"And I will give you some money to help you out a little."

"You will!" exclaimed the woman, happily. "How much?" she asked.

"A couple of thousand," suggested the man.

"Make it three," responded the woman, quickly.

"Okay, but that's all. I don't want to hear from you again, afterwards," stated the man.

Inside the woman the small child was filled with fear and was calling in his heart, "Mummy, I love you, love me." The child knew within that any love that had been there was going fast, and the child began to feel lost and alone within his mother.

"When will you get rid of him?" asked the man.

"I'm already booked for tomorrow," smiled the woman.

"Why didn't you tell me?" snapped the man. "What was all that discussion about?" he asked.

"I wanted you to face your responsibility and pay for your mistake. I am paying. I have to undergo the abortion," stated the woman.

"You wanted the money, didn't you?" snarled the man.

"Yes, I deserve it," she answered.

"Well, remember, I never want to see you again," confirmed the man.

"What about me?" thought the little child, "What about me?"

For the next few hours the mother was nervous as she thought about what lay ahead and if it would hurt her, if there would be any complications for her. Inside, the fear within the little child grew, as it became colder and colder around him. Now the child felt a total absence of love, an emptiness of feelings, an aloneness.

Suddenly the child felt a movement close by and then heard voices, saying, "This won't take long, it will soon be over. Don't worry, you will be all right."

The child felt something entering the womb around him. It felt so close and the child was afraid. "Mummy, Mummy," the child called from his heart. "Mummy, I love you, I love you." Then there was an unfamiliar noise followed by intense pain as the child felt something pulling at him.

"Mummy, Mummy. Help me, Mummy," echoed in the child's heart, as he felt intense pain as the little body began to tear apart. "Mummy, I love you," were the last feelings of the little one, as he was torn apart violently by the machine inside the child's mother, and sucked out into a waste container.

A little while later, the mother came to her senses, while the nurse beside her comforted the woman, saying, "It's all over now. It wasn't so bad was it, only a little uncomfortable? You will soon be able to get back to a normal life again."

"Thank you," replied the woman, quietly. "Thank you." Then she closed her eyes to rest a little while.

A few days later, the woman met the man who had made her pregnant to collect the money promised. "I'm glad it's over and it went okay," said the man.

"So am I. I thought there would be more pain, but it wasn't that bad. Have you got my money?" asked the woman.

"Yes. Now remember, I don't want to hear from you again," he reminded her.

"You won't, I promise," said the woman, knowing in her heart that she now detested this man.

She was given the money, and as it was handed to her, she thought for a moment she could hear a baby cry, "Mummy, that is the cost of my life." She stood silent for a moment and the man asked, "Are you all right?"

"Oh, it's nothing," said the woman, as she put the money in her bag. Again she thought she heard a little voice ask, "Am I nothing to you, Mummy?" But she dismissed the thought and said goodbye to the man, then walked away without a concern in her mind.

At that moment, a little child was in the arms of his Mother Mary in Heaven looking down on his two parents on earth. The child was crying as he saw how his mother and father had allowed their hearts of love, given by God, to be turned to hearts of stone, deceived by evil.

"I pray that God will forgive them," said the little child to Mother Mary.

"And I pray that one day love will come into their hearts again," said Mary, as she embraced the child in love.

"I love you, Mummy," said the child.

"And I love you, too," replied Mother Mary responding with the words the child had longed to hear from his parents on earth, but never did.

12/24/99 — God the Father

GOD MADE IT SO

The man was singing happily as he walked along the pathway. He was happy because he had just been informed of a promotion at work with a large salary increase. Through his mind went thoughts of how important he would be, how the extra money would mean a nicer house, a larger car, and better holidays.

"At last," he said to himself, "success is within my grasp. I deserve it, don't I!" He smiled as he thought of the long hours he had worked, the extra studying he had done, and how he had always been willing to do what his superiors had asked of him.

"What a glorious day," the man called out to no one in particular, as he walked past a group of people going in the other direction.

"Yes, it is, isn't it?" answered an older woman from the group. "But then, isn't every day?" she asked.

"What?" said the man, as his train of thought was broken.

"Every day...glorious," replied the woman.

"I suppose so," said the man with an uninterested tone in his voice, as he continued to walk on.

"It's glorious because God made it so," called the woman, now that they were some yards apart.

The man walked on, not giving another thought to what the woman had said. He returned to his dreams about what his new position would bring into his life.

"Spare a few cents for something to eat," pleaded a voice.

The man looked at the dirty hand thrust out before him, then at the person who was speaking.

"Spare some money, Sir. I have not eaten for awhile; please help me," implored the scruffy old man.

"Here," said the man as he reached into his pocket to pull out a few coins. "This is all."

"Thank you, Sir, and thank God for small mercies," said the grateful old man, "And may God bless you," he continued, as he looked at the coins in his hand. The old man knew it was not much, but with a bit of luck he could get a little more later on and afford to buy a sandwich.

"God...," thought the happy man, "Why do people keep mentioning Him?" he wondered.

"God hasn't done much for you, has He?" asked the man, who had given the money.

"Oh, He has done more than I deserve," replied the beggar, with a smile. "He brought you here today to give me this money I needed."

"The old fool," thought the happy man. "Maybe I'll give him a little more; he looks as if he needs it.

"Here, take this," the man said, as he handed some notes to the beggar.

"Why, thank you," said the poor man, as he smiled in appreciation of the gift. "You have made me the happiest man in the world today."

"Oh, come now. It is not that much," stated the man who had given the money.

"It is more than you know. Today, for the first time this week, I will be able to have a proper meal. To me it will be a banquet. How blessed I am that God sent you," replied the beggar.

"There you go, mentioning God again. He didn't send me, I came this way by my choice," explained the man.

"Whether or not you know it, God did send you, and He brought you here to bring this wonderful gift to me," insisted the beggar.

"If you say so," answered the happy man. "Enjoy your meal," he said, as he began to walk away.

"Remember, God gave me this through you. It is God Who gives us all good things," shouted the beggar to the man, who was now some distance away.

"God gives us all good things," echoed in the man's head, as he walked on. "But I worked for my good things. I got them by my hard work," he thought. The words, however, kept repeating over and over in his head. "God gives us all good things." Then the words of the woman before seemed to be there, "It's glorious because God made it so." Over and over the words continued and seemed to mix with pictures of different times in the man's life.

The man saw how he had never believed that he would make it to university, but to his and most other people's surprise, he did, and he heard, "Because God made it so." The man saw how, after university, a golden opportunity in a large prestigious company had opened for him. Again, he heard, "Because God made it so."

The man saw how he had enjoyed his work and didn't mind working long hours, for to him it was fun. Again, he heard, "Because God made it so." The man saw how his superiors had asked him to do so much, because they trusted and believed in him. Again, he heard, "Because God made it so."

There seemed to be an awakening within him now, as he began to realize that all the opportunities in his life were there because God made it so, and because it was God Who gave us all good things.

"But what about the hard work I did!" he thought. Then it came to him that God had given him the capabilities to do so. *God gave us all good things,* echoed in his head, again and again.

"If God gave me all good things," mused the man, "then really, it all belongs to Him. Whatever happens in my life, whatever I achieve, it is all because God made it so."

The man walked on thinking deeply about this; then he remembered the beggar who had so little but thanked God for it. The man thought how he and his family had so much, and now would have much more, but never thanked God at all. It saddened him as he came to realize the way he had closed himself to God in his life.

"What can I do to rectify this?" he wondered. "Well, I must start to thank God from now on, for all good things in my life, because He has made it so. I think, also, I should try to bring good things to those in need, like that beggar I met. So that, like him, others will see God bringing good things into their lives through me. What a wonderful gift that would be," he thought excitedly, "that others should see the goodness of God through someone like me."

Now he began to skip happily along the pathway as he called out, "It is a glorious day...it is...and all because God has made it so."

1/2/00 — Jesus

IT'S NEVER TOO LATE

"My children cause me so much pain with the way they behave. They always seem to be in trouble; they always seem to cause me heartache. Sometimes I wonder why I bothered having children," said the woman to her friend. "I look at other families and I am jealous because many of them look happy, as if they haven't a care in the world."

"You bothered having children," replied the friend, "because you loved your husband, and in that love your children came into life."

"Well, if they were made in love, and they were, for I do love my husband, why, then, do they behave so badly?" asked the woman.

"Did you both give your children the love, the time, and the guidance they needed?" replied the friend, with a question.

"Yes, we love them and we tried to show love to them, but I have to say that gets harder each time they do something wrong. We gave the children as much time as we could, but we were both working when they were younger, so that didn't help.

"Guidance...well, we told them what was right and what was wrong, but it does not seem they took much notice!" said the woman in a despairing voice. "We did our best, but obviously it wasn't good enough," she continued.

"Did you tell them about God?" asked the friend.

"God? Why...no, we don't think much about God ourselves, and in today's world, stories about God do not seem so important," answered the woman.

"Maybe that is where you made a mistake," stated the friend.

"What do you mean?" inquired the woman, with genuine interest.

"Well, when God is in people's lives, He brings peace, security, and love. So often those who are troubled have not known these gifts of God, and that is why they are troubled," explained the friend.

"But no one talks about God today; the stories about Him seem irrelevant," said the woman.

"I think that may be why there are so many problems in people's lives today. If you think about your children, you said you tried to love them and give them time, but that you had to work to support your family. It seems that while you were away from your children, the void you left was filled by something else. Often, what happens is that void is filled with confusion and uncertainty, as the child has no parent with it to protect it from the things that can disturb a young mind."

"So, you are saying it is my own fault?" cut in the woman.

"No, not entirely your fault. The circumstances of your life played a big part in making it this way. You needed to work, didn't you? You needed money," said the friend, comfortingly.

"Yes, we couldn't have survived without it," retorted the woman. "Anyway, we had a child minder."

"Yes, but sometimes more than a child minder is needed. A child minder cannot give the children the love the parents feel for their own," explained the friend.

"What could we have done then?" asked the woman. "We had to work, we had to leave them with someone."

"This is where God comes in. If your children had been helped to understand the love God has for them and had been encouraged to open their hearts to God's love, then in those times of uncertainty, God's love in their hearts would have helped them through. In the times when they felt a little alone or missed their parents' love, God's love would have been there surrounding them with peace and security. The Spirit of God's love would be there at every moment to watch over and protect them," suggested the friend.

"But if God is there, shouldn't He be doing that anyway?" asked the woman.

"He is, He is. The difference is whether the child is helped to be aware of God being there, and then encouraged to embrace God's loving Spirit," responded the friend. "It is when they do so," she continued, "that their lives can become ones of peace, love, and security. It is when they do not, that so often the reverse is true. What may happen, also, is that as the children grow, so does the confusion. Often, the children respond to this in anger, in violence, in drugs, in abusive behavior. Often, the children show little or no respect to anyone, and often, they show hatred, not love."

"That's my two," said the woman.

"When children have not been given much guidance, this also contributes to the wrongs they embrace in their lives," stated the friend.

"We told them what was right and what was wrong," said the woman, in justification.

"Did you explain the best guidelines of all to them: the Ten Commandments?" asked the friend.

"I don't know them myself, so how could I?" shrugged the woman.

The friend looked at the woman, saying, "Well, there are no better instructions on how to live than those, for they are all about living a good life...one of love."

"I suppose you are right. I should have told them," replied the woman, sadly.

"It's not too late," suggested the friend.

"No, they're too big now," responded the woman.

"People are never too big," said the friend.

"Do you think that those happy families I see are happy because they believe in God?" asked the woman.

"I am sure that for many that is the reason, for where God is, happiness resides," said the friend.

"If only I had thought about God before; I suppose it's too late now," said the woman, despondently.

"It's never too late," replied the friend, reassuringly.

"My kids won't change now. They have been trouble for too long. Anyway, they wouldn't listen to me now," said the woman.

"You should try. Don't give up on them or yourself. You love them still, don't you?" asked the friend.

"Yes, I do. What did you mean, give up on myself?"

"Well, if you are going to bring God's stabilizing love into your children's lives, you must first bring it into yours. If you do, you will find peace in your heart, also; it's not just there for your kids...the happiness of knowing God will help you through your worries and your concerns, because you will know God loves you, and in that knowledge comes a serenity that can bring true joy.

"It is when you start to live in God's love in this way, that your life becomes an example to your children, and so if they do not listen to your words, seeing God in your life can be the key to opening them to His love, peace, joy, and happiness. To see, for some, is far more powerful than to hear," explained the friend.

"Maybe I will try. Life is so miserable at present. There does not seem to be much hope at the moment. You know, I think you are right, because when I see people coming from the Church, they all seem to be at peace, and I have always said that you are one of the happiest people I know," said the woman.

"Well, now you know the reason why. I love God and He loves me," smiled the friend.

"You're right, you know!" stated the woman. "God hasn't been in our lives, and the whole family has suffered. I think it's time we turned to God and had some hope in our lives for once."

The friend smiled as she knew the woman meant it, and knew that God in His Mercy was always willing to embrace those who had turned away from Him, if they were willing to embrace Him.

1/11/00 — Jesus

THE CRUCIFIX ON THE WALL

Lying alone in the bed, the woman thought, "If I try not to move, it will not hurt so much," then, as she took a breath, a sharp pain racked her body. "I must try to breathe less," she thought, as the pain subsided a little. Now she felt a soreness in her back from the way she was lying and she desperately wanted to move but dared not, because she did not want to feel the pain again.

"Why must it be like this?" sobbed the woman, quietly to herself. As she said this, thoughts of her past life went through her mind. She remembered the good life she had led, the parties, the holidays, the expensive clothes...all the exciting times. She then saw in her mind, the poor in the world...how they suffered, how the poor children starved and died, how the poor suffered and died, because they had no money for simple medicines.

She saw a poor child sitting with its arms outstretched pleading, "Help me," and she saw, how in her own happy life, she had given no thought to the poor. The woman realized how wrong she had been, and she began to cry.

With each sob, pain again seared through her body like a hot iron, but she made no attempt to stop crying. Instead, through her pain, she called out, "I deserve it; I have been so selfish. God, forgive me."

A nurse came quickly to the woman, asking, "Are you in pain?"

Smiling weakly back, the woman said, "No more than I deserve."

"Now, now," soothed the nurse, "I am sure you do not deserve pain. Let me give you something for it."

"No, no, I want nothing. Leave me to my pain," implored the woman.

"But I can give you something to ease the pain," said the nurse, in hope.

"I can bear it. Please, leave me alone," pleaded the woman.

The nurse looked at the patient and smiled, "Well, if you need anything, just call," she said, as she turned and walked away.

The woman thought to herself, "I can bear it, if the poor can. God forgive me, and accept my pain in atonement for my selfishness."

As she thought this, the face of her priest hearing confession came to mind. She remembered some of the penances she had been given, and wished she had listened to the priest. She saw now how some of the penances had different meanings to what she had understood before. She saw the penances were nearly always encouraging her to do acts of mercy, helping the needy...but that she had paid scant regard to them and only made a token penance. She sobbed again and the intense pain once more reverberated through her body.

At this moment, she saw again the poor child with arms outstretched, and the child changing to become Jesus, suffering on the Cross. The words, "Please don't turn away from Me," seemed to fill her mind. Now she was sobbing and sobbing with the pain building inside her, but she struggled not to cry out, in case the nurse heard her and insisted on giving her the morphine once again.

"To You, Jesus, my Lord, I offer my pain. Please somehow use this offering to help those in need. Forgive me, Lord, for my selfishness."

She thought for a moment that she saw Jesus on the Cross smiling at her, and from that smile the woman felt a peace inside her that seemed to ease the pain a little.

"Nurse," the woman called out weakly, and within a few moments the nurse was at the bedside.

"What is it, Dear?" smiled the nurse. "Can I give you something for the pain?"

"I want to see a priest," whispered the woman, because she did not have the strength to speak any louder.

"A priest?" questioned the nurse.

"Yes," was the reply.

"I'll see if Father is in the hospital," said the nurse, gently.

"Thank you," replied the woman, closing her eyes and gritting her teeth, as the pain filled her body once more.

"Are you sure you do not want some pain relief?" asked the nurse, with genuine concern.

"It will not stop me from dying, will it?" replied the woman, in an anguished voice.

"No," was the soft reply.

"Well then, leave me to experience the last days of my life in the way I want," said the woman, as her face screwed up with the pain. In her mind, again, she saw Jesus on the Cross smiling gently, and she said, "I offer it to You, Jesus, my Lord. Forgive me, a sinner."

Shortly, the priest arrived and the woman looked at him with tears running from her eyes.

"Father, will you please hear my confession. It's not too late to confess, is it, Father?" she asked, in hope.

"Oh, my dear, it is never too late to confess. Jesus loves you and He offers forgiveness to all who repent, no matter what time in their life it is," responded the priest, as he held the woman's hand.

She squeezed his hand tightly as her body arched in pain. "Oh, God, forgive me," she cried.

"He will; I promise you, my child," said the priest.

"But Father, I am near to death and I am now confessing because of that, and if so, how can God forgive me?" asked the woman, who now lay in an exhausted but pain-free state for a moment.

"God's mercy cannot be understood by us mere mortals, my dear, but God has promised that if a sinner repents, the sinner will be forgiven.

God did not put any time limits on that promise. Now, my dear, tell me your sins, so I can give you absolution," encouraged the priest.

"Oh, Father, there have been so many, but I think the worst are my selfishness, my turning away from those in need, and my not listening to God's call in my life. I have lived a good life while others suffered, and I thought nothing of it. God forgive me, for surely this is ignoring God's Commandment to love one another."

Again, at the end of her sentence, pain filled her body and through her tears, she cried, "God, please forgive me, a sinner. I am sorry for offending You."

"My child, I absolve you of your sins," said the priest and continued with the words of absolution. The priest finished with a blessing, but the woman asked, with confusion in her voice, "Father, you didn't give me a penance."

"My dear, offer your suffering now to Jesus on the Cross, and thank Him for allowing you to do a penance through your suffering," suggested the priest.

"I will, Father. Thank you," smiled the woman, weakly.

"To You, Jesus, my Lord, I offer my pain." As she said this, she pointed to behind the priest, saying, "Father, that Crucifix on the wall is beautiful; through my pain, I will keep focused on that."

The priest turned to look behind him, but saw there was no crucifix on the wall. He smiled softly as he turned back to the woman. "Yes, you do that my dear; keep focused on the Crucifix."

"I will, Father, until death; I promise," said the woman, who then saw that the face of Jesus on the Cross was smiling gently at her. "He is smiling at me, Father, and do you know, His smile is just

141.

like yours. It's a smile of forgiveness; I know it is. Father, please, can I have Communion?" implored the woman.

"Of course, my dear," replied the priest, and then gave the dying woman the Blessed Sacrament.

"Father, my pain is gone, and so is my fear," said the now joyful woman, and then closed her eyes, saying, "My Lord," as she slipped gently into the arms of death.

The priest then said the Last Rites over the woman, whose face was still smiling...even now in death.

The nurse came over to the priest, saying, "She has gone then," with a little sadness in her voice.

"Yes, she has gone to the Lord," nodded the priest in agreement.

"Why is it that everyone who dies in this bed dies smiling?" asked the nurse.

"I think it is the Crucifix on the wall that brings them to open their hearts to true joy," said the priest.

"What Crucifix?" asked the nurse, not knowing what the priest was referring to. "There is no Crucifix on the wall here."

"Well, they all see it, and they all die happy," said the priest, "so I believe it is there."

The nurse was silent for a moment, and then said, "Well, I hope and pray that on my dying day, I will see it, too."

The priest smiled and said, "I think you will, my dear; I think you will." For at that moment over the shoulder of the nurse, the priest saw the Crucifix on the wall, with Jesus smiling softly towards the nurse, and he knew her prayer would be answered.

THE BLOOD AND TEARS

The man screamed as the knife cut into his skin, "Please stop!" but the torturer took no notice and continued with his work. The man was now writhing in agony as the knife was turned within his body to maximize the pain.

"Please stop, please!" he cried out once more through the pain.

"Will you denounce Him?" asked the torturer, again twisting the knife for effect.

"I cannot!" screamed the man again.

"Then it will continue, and it will get worse, I promise you," stated the torturer, with a grim smile.

"I cannot, no matter what you do," sobbed the man through the small respite, as the knife was withdrawn.

"You will do as I say. They all do," said the torturer matter-of-factly. "Denounce Him now and save yourself more pain." As he was saying this, the torturer showed the man the next instrument of torture he was about to use.

"I cannot. I love Him. I believe in Him and I will never betray Him," replied the man, defiantly.

"Suit yourself," said the torturer, shrugging his shoulders and then continuing with his evil work.

The screams of the man filled the air, as the well-practiced torturer inflicted greater degrees of pain. Each time the man was about to slip into unconsciousness, the torturer would stop and revive him before continuing.

"No luck with him yet?" asked a superior, who had come into the torture chamber to check on the progress being made.

"No, not yet, but I don't think it will be too long. This one doesn't like pain. I will soon break him," suggested the torturer, confidently.

"What is that he is saying?" asked the superior, as he put his ear next to the mouth of the man.

"Oh, he is praying to his God for strength, and also, he prays at times for his God to forgive me," laughed the torturer, as he inflicted more pain on the man.

"These Christians are funny people," mused the superior; "they even pray for the torturers." He looked down at the man who had tears running from his bruised eyes, and blood running from his battered lips.

"Well, don't take too long. We want him to confess there is no God, and that this man Jesus is nothing more than a story. It is important. Get on with it!" snapped the superior, as he left the room.

"You see, I have my orders," said the torturer to the man, as he stroked his hair gently.

Several hours later the superior returned, asking impatiently, "Has he agreed to denounce this myth of Jesus yet?"

"No...no. I cannot understand it. I thought he would be begging me by now to stop, and that he would say what we want, but he has not," said the torturer, with a confused look on his face.

"I have tried everything, without disfiguring him, but nothing succeeds. He is stronger than I thought."

"Well, just get him to sign a document; it does not matter if you disfigure him. Just get his signature on a confession, that he does not believe in God, and that it is all a deception to make people do as his Church asks, so it can get wealth from people," demanded the superior. He then leaned over the man, and said, as he looked into his eyes, "You will do as we ask."

The man smiled weakly back as he said, "Never," and then continued to pray.

"Take his tongue out so he can't pray!" shrieked an increasingly frustrated superior.

As the torturer came to the man's face, preparing to do his grizzly task, the man said in a whisper, "I forgive you, and I pray that God will, too."

"Listen to that!" exclaimed the torturer. "These will be his last words, and they are ones forgiving me and praying for my forgiveness. Incredible!" he said, as he forced the man's mouth open, ready to remove his tongue. He paused for a moment, as he looked into the man's eyes.

"Do it!" ordered the superior, and so the torturer followed the command.

"Will you sign now?" barked the superior to the semi-conscious man, who responded by weakly shaking his head from side to side.

"Continue!" ordered the superior. "I will return soon, and I want that signature." Then he left the room, obviously very angry.

"Well, my friend," smiled the torturer. "It does not seem you will be saying many prayers now. Come on, sign the paper, and this will end. What do you say...will you do it?" he asked.

Again the man shook his head from side to side.

"Where do you get the courage? I didn't think you would last so long," said the torturer amazed at the man's endurance. The man tapped his strapped hand on the table he was tied to, and the torturer looked down to see the man had drawn a red cross on the table from his blood.

"All you Christians talk of the Cross; I wonder how it gives you so much courage," inquired the torturer, as he placed his finger in the blood that made the cross.

At that moment, in his mind, he saw Jesus on the Cross before him. He felt Jesus say the words, "Father, forgive them, for they know not what they do." Then in his heart he felt the love of Jesus touch him from the Cross. His whole life was now before him and he knew now that God did exist, and that he had been turning from God and offending God. Now he saw the blood and water flowing from the side of Jesus to surround him, and he saw in that the blood and tears of all the Christians he had tortured and killed.

The torturer fell to his knees and began to cry as he came to know how evil his life had been, and then he saw the gates of hell opening before him and heard the words, "Unless you repent, this is what awaits you."

"Forgive me, Jesus," cried the torturer, not from the fear of seeing hell, but from the pain he now felt at hurting God.

"Forgive me...forgive me," he sobbed.

Then he remembered the man on the table and jumped to his feet to begin undoing the straps that bound the man.

"Forgive me. I am sorry," he spluttered, as he helped the man from the table.

The man could hardly stand, but he looked at his torturer and smiled weakly, as he nodded his head as if to say, "I do."

The tortured man, in his mind, was now thanking God for touching the heart of the torturer. Through his pain, the man had not only prayed for the torturer's forgiveness, but also for his coming to know the truth of God, and the man's prayers had been answered.

The torturer turned to look at the man, and cried, "Please baptize me. I know this is what makes a person a Christian. Well, I want to be Jesus' now and forever."

The man shrugged his shoulder as if to say, "How?"

"What do you need?" asked the torturer, as he gave the man a pen and piece of paper to write on. The man wrote: Water and my prayer book.

"I'll get them. Wait here," said the torturer, as he sat the man down and rushed out of the room to return a short while later with a bowl of water and the prayer book, which he had retrieved from the rubbish tin near the cells.

"Do you need this, as well?" asked the torturer, as he held out his hand to show the priest's collar he had also recovered. The man nodded and smiled, then put the collar around his neck, blessed the water, and indicated to the torturer to kneel. He then said the words of Baptism in his mind, as he poured some of the water over the still sobbing torturer. After the makeshift baptism, the priest embraced his torturer, but then had to sit before he nearly fainted from the terrible pain he still could feel. The torturer knelt before him with head bowed, saying over and over, "Forgive me. I am sorry. Will God forgive me?"

The priest smiled as he nodded in confirmation, and then took the paper and pen, writing: In your Baptism, you have been washed clean of your sins, and in the love of God, I forgive you.

As the priest blessed the man, the torturer felt a peace come upon him with the truth of these words. It was at this moment, the superior returned to the room.

"What is going on here?" shouted the superior, as he saw the torturer kneeling before the priest with his collar on, and the priest slowly and weakly making the Sign of the Cross over the torturer's head.

"I...I...I," stuttered the torturer, as he turned his head to look at the superior.

"You are supposed to be getting him to denounce his God, but here he is wearing that stupid collar. Look!" he shrieked; "he even has his prayer book! What are you doing?"

The torturer stood up facing his superior saying, "I gave them to him."

"You did! Why?" barked the angry superior.

"He is right in what he believes. I know he is, for I now, too, believe in Jesus. Jesus is my Lord and my God," replied the torturer with a peaceful look on his face.

"Snap out of it and get on with your job, or you will be suffering with him!" ordered the superior.

"I don't care. I love God," said the smiling torturer, who was now feeling a happiness within, that he had never known before.

"Guards!" bellowed the superior two or three times, before the sound of the guards' heavy footsteps could be heard running down the corridor towards him.

"Arrest him!" snapped the superior, pointing to the torturer, as the guards rushed into the room. The torturer looked at the priest, who smiled gently back at him, with blood running from his now tongueless mouth.

"You will suffer with him!" snarled the superior, as the guards grabbed the torturer and the priest. "Strap them both to the tables!" ordered the superior.

As they were both pushed to the tables, the priest reached out to touch his former torturer, and as their hands touched, the torturer looked into his new friend's eyes, knowing that soon it would not be the end for both of them, but the beginning of a new life with God.

1/22/99 — Jesus

SHARING A MEAL

"Daddy, why do we always have to say a prayer before we eat?" asked the child, at the dinner table.

"Well, it is to thank God for the food He gives us to eat," replied the father to his child, with a smile.

"But Daddy, it takes so long and I am hungry," wailed the little one.

"Your father leads us in prayer at each meal so that we don't forget God and His love for us," cut in the mother. "It is a way of saying to God that we love Him."

"Now, let us join hands and pray," suggested the father, as he reached across the table to hold his wife and child's hands.

The child closed her eyes tightly as if concentrating deeply, and the look on her face made both parents smile. The three of them together then prayed to God in thanks for the meal before them. At the end of the prayer, after saying, "Amen," the little girl still had her eyes closed tightly.

"You can open your eyes now," said the mother to her child.

"I don't want to just yet. I am still praying," replied the girl.

"I thought you were hungry?" questioned the father.

"I am, but I want to just say a little more to God," answered the child, with a serious look on her face.

"It will get cold," reminded the mother, gently. "Don't take too long."

"I won't. I've nearly finished," said the girl.

The father smiled at his wife and shrugged his shoulders, and as he did so, their daughter said out loud, "Amen," and then she began to eat her food slowly.

When the parents noticed a few minutes later that the child had stopped eating and yet there was still about half of the meal left on her plate, the mother asked, "Aren't you well, Dear? You haven't finished your meal. It's your favorite, as well."

"I am not sick, Mummy," answered the girl, quietly.

"What is it then, Dear?" asked the concerned mother.

"I am not hungry now. Can you put it in a box for me?" asked the child.

"A box? It's not a restaurant," said the father, with a smile.

"Anyway, I thought you said you were hungry, yet you have hardly eaten anything," continued the father.

"I was, but I am not, now," replied the little girl, with a serious look on her face. "But you could put it in a box for me."

"How about if I put it on a plate in the refrigerator?" suggested the mother, as she began to rise from her seat to take the food from the table. "You could come into the kitchen and eat it later if you are hungry."

"No, Mummy, it's not for me," said the girl in reply.

"Who is it for then, Dear?" asked a now curious mother.

"It is for the poor," answered the girl.

"The poor!" exclaimed the father.

"Yes, Daddy, the poor. When I was praying before dinner, I was hungry, but then while I had my eyes closed, I saw a picture of lots of children who were very hungry, hungrier than I am. I want to give some of my food to them," explained the child, with an innocent expression on her face.

"Oh, the poor," said the mother, as she looked at her husband, with a gentle smile of understanding on her face.

"Well, by the time this food got to them, it would be bad and they couldn't eat it, so why don't you finish it, Dear?" suggested the mother.

"But what about the poor?" questioned the girl. "They are hungry, too."

"Well, what we will do is send them some money so they can buy food," said the father, as he stood up and went to his daughter, putting his arm around her shoulders to give her a hug. "It is good that you think of the poor and want to help them," he said.

"God showed me I should," said the daughter, matter-of-factly.

"What did He show you?" asked the father.

"Daddy, when I saw the children hungry, as I prayed, I saw the food on my plate, and then Jesus saying to me, 'Share with them,'" explained the little girl.

"I promise you, we will send money to help them," said the amazed father, as he again looked at his wife who nodded in agreement, as she said, "We will, my dear. I promise."

"You will send them lots of money, won't you Daddy?" asked the girl.

The father looked at his daughter, and as he did, he saw in her, now, one of the starving children often shown on TV. He stood there silently for a moment, with tears running from his eyes at the sight of the starving child before him.

"Why are you crying, Daddy? Mummy, why are you crying, too?" asked the child, with a worried sound in her voice.

At that moment, the vision of the starving child was gone, and the father once more saw his daughter in front of him. He turned to look at his wife, who still had tears on her cheeks.

"Did you see that child, too?" asked the husband of his wife, who nodded in silent agreement.

"Daddy, why is Mummy so sad?" asked the child again.

"I think we just saw one of the hungry children, too," replied the father.

"You did?" smiled the child. "We will help them, won't we?" Together, both the mother and father nodded their heads in agreement.

"Yes, we will," said the mother, with a certainty in her voice. Then, with her husband, she sat down and they began to work out exactly how much money they could send each week for the poor.

"It's not much, but it is all we can afford," said the husband.

"Daddy, give them my allowance," suggested the little girl.

"That will not be necessary, Dear," smiled the mother.

"But I want them to have it," insisted the daughter.

"How about you have half and the poor have half," suggested the father. "Then you will still have some for yourself."

"Okay, Daddy," replied the girl, but she knew in her mind that she would put the other half in her moneybox and send it to the poor when she had collected a lot.

"If only everyone would send what they could afford, there wouldn't be any poor," stated the mother, sadly.

"Why don't they?" asked the daughter.

"Before you prayed at dinner, did you think of the poor children?" asked the father.

"No, Daddy, I didn't," replied the daughter, looking somewhat guilty.

"Most people don't either; they seem to be blind to the poor. I was, and so was your mother, before we prayed tonight. When you prayed and saw the hungry children, it made you want to help them; and, when you told us about it, we, too, saw a hungry child, and that made us want to help. By your prayers tonight, that blindness was taken from all of us, and from now on I think we should pray that blindness is taken from others as well," he said, not only for his daughter's sake, but for his own and his wife's sake, also.

"Daddy, maybe I should tell other people about my prayers and what I saw," suggested the girl.

"Yes, Dear that would be a good thing to do. It might help others to see, like your mother and I did tonight," replied the father, encouragingly.

"When I go to bed tonight, I am going to pray hard that everyone helps the poor," said the little girl.

"Remember," said the mother, "what happened in your prayers at dinner, and pray that when others pray, it happens to them, too."

"I will, Mummy. I am going to bed to pray now," said the girl, as she came to her parents to kiss them good night.

"And you didn't want to pray at dinner," smiled the father.

"I am glad we did, Daddy," she said, as she left the room to go to bed and pray.

"How much can we give?" asked the wife of her husband.

"Only one or two dollars a week. Any more, and we won't have enough for ourselves," he replied, sadly.

"Maybe you will get a job soon and we can afford to give more," said the wife, in hope.

The husband looked at his wife and replied, with a smile, "I promise you this, the more we get, the more we will give to the poor. I promise you, and I promise God." He then took his wife's hand and said, "Let's say a prayer that God, in His goodness, will help us to help others."

As they prayed, neither one of them thought about the difficult times they had had over the past years, as they could not find work and had to survive on the little help the government gave to them. Instead, they thought about the starving children in the world and what they could do to help, while not far away a family with plenty was sitting down to its meal with no thought of the poor or of the needy, only thoughts of their good life. As they were about to begin the meal, their little daughter said, "Daddy, why do we always have to say a prayer before we eat?"

There, standing at the side of the table, unseen by the family, stood Jesus, waiting for these hearts to open in prayer, so that they, too, could come to see the poor in the world, and have that longing in their hearts to help them.

1/23/00 — Jesus

A PRIDEFUL MAN

The man was sitting alone in the church thinking of his life. He thought of the good things he had done, and he thought of the bad things he had done. He then placed in his mind a set of scales, and on one side of the scales he placed the good he had done, and on the other, the bad. No matter how he tried, the man could not get the scales to weigh in favor of the good; the bad always seemed heavier.

He began to feel a little sad and, as he looked at his life, he became disappointed with it and with himself. He looked at his life, and thought, "I will never overcome the bad; it seems always to have been with me and it weighs so heavy on me. I feel it will break my heart."

As he reflected on his life, he remembered what his father had said to him as a boy. "Son, there will always be temptation in your life, and there will always be the opportunity to sin, for in your humanity, there is a weakness that opens us to sin."

He remembered asking his father, "What can we do to stop sinning, then, Father, and what is this weakness? How can we overcome it?"

"Son," replied the father, "the weakness all people have is their pride. It is in pride people's hearts are opened to many sins, and it is in pride many lives are damaged. To overcome pride is impossible in yourself. The moment you believe you can overcome your pride by yourself, is the moment your pride wins, and you are on the path that leads to certain defeat. It is when a person says, "I am weak, I cannot win," and the person turns to God, asking for His help, that by God's grace, the person begins to walk the path of assured success.

"Remember, Son, in yourself is weakness; in God is strength. In those moments, when you feel life is so heavy, when you feel you are being dragged into a dark hole you cannot get out of, in those moments, do not rely on yourself or you may find you are dragged even further down. In those moments, turn to God and ask for His help, and He will help you; I promise you, He will. Son, try to remember this and turn to God, asking Him to help, and when you do, remember your old father who gave you this advice. It is the same advice my father gave to me, and it has saved me many times. It is good advice."

The picture of his father telling him this faded from his mind, and as it did he said, quietly, "Thank you, Dad." The man then looked at the altar before him, and said out loud, "God, please help me; I cannot do it by myself. I have committed so many sins, and yet I've done so little good. Please help me, Jesus, to do better."

Then the man knelt down and began to pray over and over, "Forgive me, Lord...a prideful man."

The more he prayed the stronger he felt inside. Now he saw the scales before him again. It was still weighing heavily on the side of bad, but then he saw a hand tip the scales in favor of the good, and he heard the words, "In My eyes, you are not as bad as you are in your own, and there is still time in your life to do much more good."

The man began to cry, as he continued to pray from his heart, "Forgive me, Lord...a prideful man." The strength he now felt inside of him was so intense, he knew God was showing him that God was there for him to lean on. Understanding this, the man also began to feel a deep joy and a deep peace.

"Lord," he said, out loud... "I will do my best from now on to do good and to please You, but I will always need Your strength. I cannot do it by myself, for I am weak."

The man heard again inside his head a voice saying, "I will always be there for you." The man smiled, knowing this was the truth, and knowing that ahead of him, by the grace of God, lay the opportunity to do good in his life.

"Son," called the father, into the Church. "You had better get ready; we will have to leave soon for the cathedral. You don't want to be late for your ordination, do you?"

"No, I don't," smiled the man, as he got up and walked out of the Church. He went over to his father embracing him, saying, "Thank you, Dad."

WHEN THE TIME COMES

"The clock seems to move so quickly," said the woman to the person in the room with her. "I never have known time to go so fast."

"Relax if you can; watching the clock is not going to make time go any slower. It will just make you more anxious," replied the other woman in the room.

"I can't help it; it will soon be time, and I can't seem to do anything except to watch time while I wait. Funny isn't it, I didn't think too much about time before," mused the woman.

"Are you sure there is nothing I can get for you?" asked the other.

"Will the priest be here soon?" replied the first woman, questioningly.

"He is on his way. He shouldn't be too long," confirmed the other.

"He is a kind man. He brings me great comfort," said the woman, with a smile.

"Priests do that, don't they?" agreed the other.

"He keeps telling me God loves me and cares for me; that Jesus will be with me when the time comes," explained the woman. She continued, "I will go to confession and receive Communion beforehand, and he tells me my soul will be cleansed and then filled with Jesus, so I will be in a state of grace for whatever happens. I know it's true, so really, I shouldn't be afraid, should I? But I am a little."

"Try to be strong. Lean on Jesus; He will carry you through," said the priest, who had just entered the room, as the woman was saying this.

"Father, you're here. I'm glad," smiled the woman. "I was waiting for you."

"My child, I am glad to be with you, for your courage and faith in this difficult time strengthens me, you know," stated the priest, as he gave the woman a gentle hug.

"Will you hear my confession now, Father?" asked the woman, nervously.

"Of course, my child, and after that I will celebrate Mass for you," replied the priest, as he took his stole out of his case.

"Will you give us a few moments alone please?" asked the priest of the other woman.

"I will be just outside the door, if you need me," she replied as she got up and walked through the doorway.

After the confession was over, the priest called the other woman back into the room, saying, "Do you want to join our Mass?"

"Yes, please, Father; it would be a privilege," she replied, looking at the now peaceful woman who had just confessed her sins.

"You seem at peace," she said to her.

"I am. It is good to confess all your sins. It is as if a weight has been lifted from me," responded the woman.

When the Mass had finished, all three of them sat there quietly for some time, reflecting on the Sacrament they had just received. The other woman looked at the clock and jumped up, saying, "Look at what time it is. We had better get you ready; they will be coming for you soon."

"Father, will you stay with me until they take me away?" asked the first woman, with still a little fear showing in her voice.

"I will, of course. God love you, my child," answered the priest.

Within a short time, the woman had changed into a gown and lay down on the bed in her room. The other woman came over with a syringe in her hand saying, "I will give you this; it will relax you and make you sleepy before they come."

"Thank you, Sister," said the woman, as she held out her arm to the nurse.

"Father," said the woman, looking at the priest. "I know Jesus is with me, and I know whatever the outcome, I am safe."

The priest smiled gently at the woman, now slipping into her drug-induced sleep, and said, "You always were, and you always will be."

A few moments later, when they came and took the woman to the operating room, the priest asked the nurse, "There is not much hope, then?"

"No, Father; the tumor is so large, it is unlikely she will survive the operation, but if she does, she will be incapacitated for the rest of her life.

The doctors give only a 10% chance of success, so I doubt if she will come through the operation," explained the nurse.

"That's a shame," said the priest. "She had a promising future as a nun; you could see it, even though she has only been a sister for less than a year. Anyway, she is safe with God now...let's leave it to Him."

The nurse nodded in agreement, and then said to the priest, "In life, she is God's, and if she dies, in death she will be His, too. That's a happy thought to hold onto, isn't it, Father?"

"Yes, my child, it is. A happy thought I would like to have about all people," suggested the priest, as he said in his mind, "If only, Lord...if only."

2/6/00 — Jesus

ALL PEOPLE MUST BE BEAUTIFUL

As the sun was setting, a man looked at the sky and said to himself, "What a beautiful sunset." He sat down thinking on the sight before him, and how nothing mankind made compared to the beauty he was now seeing. Then, in a moment, it came to him that whoever created such beauty must have a beautiful heart from which it came. Then he realized that, of course, it was God Who had created the sunset, and that God must have a beautiful heart. As this thought continued, he came to realize that God must be true beauty, and that God must be the creator of all that is beautiful. In his mind he saw all the different peoples of the world, and came to understand that God had created them all, and that being so, all people must be beautiful.

At that moment, he stood up and reached to his sleeve to tear off the swastika that was on it, saying out loud, "How can I hate anyone, for all are beautiful gifts of God's love." He decided there and then, that no longer would he listen to the words of hate from his leaders, and no longer would he see anyone, regardless of race, as less than he.

The man walked home smiling and feeling a peace within him, a peace that would carry him through the torture and death that lay ahead of him for rejecting the creed of his SS masters; a peace that would bring him to God's glory in Heaven through his martyrdom.

2/21/00 — Jesus

DIVINE HANDS

When the door opened, the man saw before him the smiling face of his wife.

"You're home dear!" she exclaimed, as she reached out and put her arms around him.

"Yes, at last," replied the man with a sigh of relief, as he felt the warmth and love of his wife touching him.

"It has been a long time, but now you are home," said the wife into her husband's ear, with the tenderness of love in each word that said she meant it. The two of them stood in the doorway for a few minutes, just embracing each other and saying no more.

"Dad," called out a voice from within the house. "Dad, are you there?"

"Yes, Son, I'm home," answered the father. "I'm coming," he said, as his wife let go of him and the man rushed down the passageway. Turning into the first room, the man saw his son lying in the bed that was there.

"Dad!" shouted the child, excitedly with his arms outstretched waiting for a hug. The man reached down into the bed and put his powerful arms around his son, and lifted him out of the bed, holding the boy close to him.

"Dad," said the child, "I am glad you are home. I missed you."

The man kissed his son on the cheek saying, "So am I, Son, and I missed you, too."

"You will not go away again, will you, Dad?" asked the child, with an almost pleading tone in his voice.

"No, Son, I promise I will not leave you again," replied the father, with conviction.

"He is tired from all the excitement," explained the woman to her husband. "He has been waiting all day for you. He didn't eat anything because he was worried you were not coming."

"Son, you must eat or you will get sick," said the man.

"Dad, I am sick," reminded the child.

"Sorry, I didn't think," stated the father, as he shook his head from side to side, thinking how stupid he was to say that. "Anyway, Son, why don't you eat a little with me now? I'm starving hungry, and if your mother has some food, I would like to fill my stomach with her good cooking." The man said this, as he lay the boy back into bed, and gently smiled at his wife.

"Of course, Dear, there is plenty of food. It's been waiting for you to come home and eat it, and you certainly look as if you need it," smiled the wife, as she looked at her husband's body which had lost all the excess weight that was there before he left home.

"Yes, Dad," added the son, "you've lost a lot of weight; you had better eat something before you waste away." The father, with tears forming in his eyes, looked at his son, who was wasting away from his sickness.

"Dad, it was a joke; don't cry," explained the son, as he weakly leaned over to stroke his father's face, comforting him.

The wife quickly left the room to return a few moments later, saying out loud, "Chicken pie," as she held before her a freshly baked pie.

"Dad, Mom's made your favorite," said the sick boy, encouragingly, to his still crying father. "We can eat some together."

"Yes, Son, let's enjoy it," replied the man, as he wiped the tears away.

As the three of them shared the meal, the wife kept looking at her husband, saying several times, "I love you, and I am glad you are home," while the son just ate quietly looking at his father with eyes that said, "I have missed you."

After a while, the son spoke up, saying, "Dad, you won't leave us again, will you? Mom is going to need you, and you are going to need her."

The father smiled at his son, and then replied, "I will never leave again, I promise." Both the son and the wife beamed with happiness at these words.

When the meal was over, the child said to both of his parents, "Let us say a Rosary together like we used to." All three then joined in prayer as a family.

After the prayers, the father said, "I always feel good after I pray. It is what kept me going in prison...that and the talks with the priest. Oh, and of course, your visits, Dear," he said, as he looked at his wife and took her hand.

"I am sorry I couldn't come more," said the wife, with a sadness in her voice, "but it was very hard to."

"I know, Dear; you needed to stay home and look after our son," replied the husband, with understanding.

"I couldn't come to see you at all. I am sorry, Dad," apologized the son.

"You have nothing to be sorry about. It was my fault I was in prison, not yours," stated the man.

"But you did it because of me," cut in the sick son.

"Your being sick is no excuse for my breaking the law. There is no excuse for sin," explained the man firmly.

"Anyway, you are home now," smiled the wife, as she squeezed her husband's hand.

"Home to stay!" said the son.

"We had better give you some peace now, so you can rest," suggested the mother, gently, as she rose and went to make her son comfortable in the bed.

"Those prayers were good, Dad," said the son. "I hope we can say many more together."

"So do I, Son," answered the father, as he rose, kissed his son, and said, "Sleep now," before leaving the room with his wife, who turned the lights out as she left.

Then in the other room, as they sat together, the husband began to explain his time in prison.

"I missed you both; it was hard not being able to see your faces, to talk to you, to touch you, and to be with you. I deserved my punishment, for I was foolish, but both of you suffered, also, because of my stupidity, and that hurts me even more than the imprisonment."

"It wasn't all your fault," soothed his wife, "and you were driven by necessity and desperation to crime. You did it for us, I know, and so I think it was fitting that we, too, should suffer a little."

"You know, every day in prison I prayed for God to forgive me for hurting that man. I never meant for anyone to get hurt; it was very unfortunate. At first I didn't think God would forgive me, as I kept seeing the pain I caused. It was only when I spoke to the priest in confession and told him everything, that I came to understand God would forgive me.

"Father told me that Jesus loved me, and that, yes, even though I had sinned, Jesus continued to love me and continued to offer me His forgiving grace from the Cross. Father reminded me that Jesus knew in my heart I loved Him, that Jesus knew why I had sinned, and that Jesus knew I was sorry. He said that did not make the sin right, for no matter what the reason, no sin is acceptable to God, and that no sin should be acceptable to mankind.

"It took some time for me to understand and accept what Father said, but when I prayed each night, I seemed to find a strengthening as I thought on Father's words, until one night I knew... I just knew, God did love me and God did forgive me."

The man paused for a moment and smiled gently to his wife, who just sat there quietly waiting for him to continue.

"When I hurt that man, I was so desperate I could only think of our son suffering, and I wanted to do something to stop the pain. We couldn't afford the medicine, and there did not seem to be anyone to help us. I was so afraid for our son, and I even thought God had turned from us, as none of our prayers seemed to be answered. I was angry at God and I should not have been.

"Father said many people react this way in their pain, but that God in His love does not stop loving them. Father said I should not feel guilty about this anymore, for it was a moment of weakness that brought this anger at God into my life. Father said the important thing is that I have returned to loving God and stopped blaming God for the problems in my life. That I should recognize that God makes everything good for mankind, and it is mankind, in its weaknesses, that changes this.

"If only I could have controlled my fear and anger at that time, things would have been so different. When I went to the hospital to steal the medicine, and that doctor tried to stop me, all I could think was to get the medicine for our son. I lashed out. I know I should not have done that. I didn't mean for him to get hurt. I mean, I fractured his skull with the medicine bottle in my hand. How easy it was to sin, to steal, to hurt another...how easy.

"All it brought was more pain; it didn't help at all. Father said that is what sin does; it never helps, it only makes matters worse, even though at times you may not see this."

"It's true, Dear," agreed the wife; "sin brings only more suffering; it never makes things better."

"That doctor in a coma for so long...it must have caused his family a lot of concern. I thank God he is all right now," said the husband, with relief in his voice. "The doctor's family suffered, we suffered, and all because of my despair, my anger, and my sin."

"Well, it is over now; you have paid your debt, and as you said, thank God, the doctor is all right. Now though, you have got to put the past behind you, and start living with hope for the future," encouraged the wife, as she again squeezed her husband's hand.

"I am going to try my best to make it up to both of you. I am going to make every day a day to be thankful for. From now on, I am going to make our son happy every day...wait and see," responded the husband, excitedly.

"You know, he only has a few months left now," reminded the wife.

"I know, and I am going to make them good for him, with your help and by the grace of God. You know, I learned in prison that if you give every day to God, no matter what happens, it is a good day."

The wife smiled at her husband, and in her heart was a happiness that the man she loved had come to find a deeper relationship with God through his anguish and imprisonment.

Just then, there was a knock on the door.

"I'll get it," said the husband, as he rose and went down the passageway to open the house door.

"You're home, then," said the smiling man who stood outside.

"It's you. I...uh," stuttered the released prisoner.

"It's good to see you. May I come in?" asked the still smiling visitor.

"Of course," replied the man, with a little confusion and uncertainty in his voice.

"The doctor has visited us often while you were away," said the wife, as she stood behind her husband and put her hand on his shoulder. "He has been bringing medicine and treating our son without charging us anything. He has been so kind."

"But I nearly killed you, Doctor," said the man, bowing his head in shame.

"You acted in desperation. In the same situation, I probably would have acted in a similar way," replied the doctor.

"I am sorry for what I did to you. Please forgive me," pleaded the man.

"I have already," smiled the doctor.

"I needed to say that I am sorry, and I needed to hear you say that you forgave me. Thank you, Doctor," continued the man, with his head still bowed, "and thank you for being so kind to my family. I thought you would be angry, but instead you are kind. How can I ever repay you?"

"There is nothing to repay. You know, when you hit me, my whole life changed. Before that, I used to think those with no money were a burden on society, and I used to ignore them. My patients were always wealthy, and I used to treat them for often minor ailments and charge them high prices, but I was never happy in my work.

"After you hit me, I spent a lot of time recovering in bed, and it gave me a chance to think about life. I started to realize how empty my life was, even with all the money I had. I certainly did not enjoy my work or feel fulfilled by it. My family life also seemed a little empty, as usually we were only thinking about ourselves and our comfort.

"As I lay in bed, I began to think about you and why you would strike me. At first I was angry, but then I thought there must have been something that drove you to do this. One day your wife came to visit me, and she explained your situation...

how your son was sick and you were desperate to get medicine for him, but you could not afford it. As she said this, I thought of my son, and I wondered what I would have done if I were you. I am sure I would have taken the medicine as you did. Now I am only sorry I disturbed you, and that in your fear of not being able to help your son, you struck out at me. I know you didn't mean it.

"Your wife kindly left me a Bible to read, and the words in it touched me deeply. I had read these words before, but then they meant nothing; now, however, they were coming alive. As I read, I saw how wrong it was that some should suffer in poverty or in need, while others had plenty. I decided to spend some of my time treating those who did not have much and maybe could not afford expensive medicines or treatment.

"Your wife graciously accepted my help, and also put me in contact with others who needed help. So, now I spend half my time with the wealthy, and half my time with the needy, and I have found that my life has never been so happy. So, I should thank you and your wife for that," suggested the doctor, genuinely.

"How is your son tonight?" asked the doctor.

"He is tired from the excitement of his dad coming home," replied the wife. Then she led the doctor into the son's room, followed by her husband. The doctor went over to the son and began to feel his pulse, and then to examine his body in various places, doing it so gently, he did not disturb the boy from his sleep. When he had finished, they went into the adjoining room, and the father asked, "Is it true he has only a little time left?"

The doctor smiled as he nodded his head, "Yes, not long now. Maybe two or three months." The wife offered the doctor some coffee, which he accepted, and sat down at the table with both of them.

"There is nothing that can be done?" asked the husband.

"Nothing. I am sorry," confirmed the doctor. "It's all in God's hands now."

"Then he is in good hands," smiled the wife, and the others nodded in agreement.

"They are the same hands I felt around me while I was in hospital," added the doctor. "And they brought me comfort and great strength."

"And they are the same hands I felt around me in prison, and they, too, brought me comfort and great healing," concurred the husband.

"And they are the same hands that kept me secure in my lonely moments. The hands that brought you, doctor, to help with my son. The hands that brought my husband home safe, and the hands that gave both of you new hearts... hearts which bring joy to mine and make my heart one that thanks God for His goodness in my life," said the wife.

"Mom, Dad," came the cry from the next room, and all three rushed in to see what was wrong.

"What is it, Son?" asked the father, as he went over to his smiling son and held him.

"I saw two hands in the air and they were lifting me up," said the still smiling boy. "It was real. They were here, but as soon as I called you, they disappeared."

The husband, wife, and doctor looked at each other and were silent, until the boy said, "And I heard a nice voice say, 'Soon you will be in My hands forever, and you will be happy.' I wish those hands would stay forever," said the boy.

The wife looked at her husband, and as tears streamed down her cheeks, said to her son, "They are the best hands to be in...the best."

Then she, too, embraced him, while the doctor stood there nodding in agreement and praying in his heart, that he, too, would one day come to be in those divine hands forever.

·

2/27/00 — Jesus

HAVE FAITH

"It is amazing!" exclaimed the doctor, as he held the newly born baby in his hands. "Every time I deliver a baby, I am filled with wonder over the new life that has come to earth," he continued, as he held the child in front of its mother.

"You have a beautiful baby girl; a blessing from God." The mother looked at her child and smiled, nodding weakly in agreement, reaching out for her baby, which she then held close to her.

"She is beautiful, Doctor," said the husband and father, who was also there in the room. "Look at her little hands and feet; they are wonderful."

The doctor looked once more at the baby girl, then back at the man, saying, "You are a lucky man. You should thank God for His blessings in your life."

"I will, Doctor, everyday; I promise," replied the man.

"You know, I have delivered thousands of babies. Each time, I look at the child and wonder what God has planned for them to do in their lives, and I wonder if the child will be given the opportunity, help, love, and encouragement to respond to God's call," pondered the doctor.

"We will give her every opportunity. This is a promise we made to God before she was born, and it is one we intend to keep," responded the father.

"I am pleased to hear that, and I will pray you will be able to do so. I meet so many parents who make promises to God before their child is born, but do not keep them. I hope you do," said the doctor. He then continued, "You know, God has given you a wonderful gift, and with that gift comes the responsibility to help your child live as God wants her to. If she can do that, her life will be a happy one, and I know that is what you want for her...to be happy."

The father smiled at the doctor and moved to the side of the bed and began to stroke both the head of his wife and his daughter, saying, "This is what we both want...that she is happy." As he did this, the father could feel and hear little sounds of what seemed like contentment coming from his newly born daughter.

His wife opened her eyes and looked with happiness at her husband. "We did it," she whispered; "we did it."

The doctor said, as he left the room, "I will come back later. You should have time together now."

The wife, still looking at her husband and smiling, said weakly, "I knew she would be all right. I knew God would hear and answer our prayers."

The husband, with joy in his face, replied, "Yes, God did, and everything is fine."

The mother leaned forward and kissed her baby softly on the forehead. "If you have faith, all is possible," she said.

The man stood there silently just thinking about all the difficulties in the pregnancy. Thinking about the other doctors who advised them to terminate the pregnancy, because they thought the mother would die. Thinking about the strength of faith his wife had to say no to an abortion, no matter what the risk. Thinking about the way his wife would tell them all, that God would take care of her family, and if she were to die so that her baby could live, then that, too, was God's will, and she would accept it.

Thinking about the times he felt so weak and so helpless believing his wife might die, but how always she would say, "Have faith." Thinking how they found, through the Church, a doctor who shared their belief, their faith...a doctor who helped them through the hard times they faced... a doctor who knew God would do the best in this situation, and a doctor who treasured life, as it is supposed to be.

"What are you thinking about, Dear?" asked the wife, interrupting the man's train of thought.

"About how strong you are, my love," he replied, tenderly.

"We are both strong by the grace of God," said the wife, lovingly, as she looked at her husband, with admiration in her eyes.

"And I think our daughter is, also," laughed the man as the baby squeezed his finger which he had placed in her hand. Just then the doctor returned, "Have you thought of a name for her yet?" he asked. Both the husband and wife smiled, as they said simultaneously, "Faith."

HEARTS THAT LOVE GOD

It was early in the morning when the man awoke and could not get back to sleep. He lay there trying not to move too much, so as not to disturb his sleeping wife. He turned to look at her and smiled, as he thought how happy she had made him in their married life.

He thought of how young she was when they first got married. How, through their marriage, there had been many ups and downs, many good times, and many difficult times. He remembered how his wife always said in the good times, to thank God for them, and how in the difficult times, she said to ask God to give them the strength to thank Him for those, too. He smiled as he thought of the expressions on her face when she would say this; expressions he loved.

"Are you awake, Dear?" he heard his wife ask.

"Yes, I am. I hope I didn't wake you," he replied, with concern.

"No, you didn't," she said, as she turned to embrace him. "I couldn't sleep, and I was just lying here thinking about our life together."

"So was I," responded the husband.

"I was thinking how God has been good to us, and how you never forgot that, Dear," explained the wife, gently.

"I was thinking the same about you!" exclaimed the surprised husband. "Isn't it strange how we thought the same thing?"

"Not at all, Dear," replied the wife, as she squeezed her husband. "Hearts that love God are often in tune with each other."

"Yes, we often have been, haven't we?" said the husband, thinking about the past.

"And we will continue to be," confirmed the wife. Then as they lay there embracing each other, both slipped into sleep again with thoughts of their life together on their minds.

As they slept, the door to the bedroom opened quietly, and a man looked in on the sleeping couple, closing the door to return to his own bedroom, where his wife was sitting up in the bed.

"Are they all right?" she asked.

"Yes, Dear," replied the man. "They are both asleep with smiles on their faces."

"I hope we can be as happy as my grandparents when we have been married as long as they have," said the woman.

"Yes, 60 years of marriage, and they are so in love," stated the man.

"Come to bed, Dear, and let's say a little prayer together that our marriage can be like theirs," suggested the wife.

"I think it is all the prayers they have said through the years that have helped them stay in love."

"Well, if that's so, we better make sure we pray every day, because I want to stay in love with you," smiled the husband.

"And I with you," replied the woman, and then the two of them joined in prayer asking God to help them love each other eternally...a prayer that was heard and would be answered...a prayer that would be answered for all those who said it and meant it.

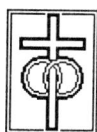

THE GREATEST LOVE OF ALL

"Do you think it's true?" asked the man of his friend. "Do you think it's Him?" he continued.

"I don't know. Some say He is, while others say He is not," answered the friend.

"If it was Him, surely He would not let them do this to Him?" wondered the man.

"Who knows what God's plan is for anyone?" said the friend, as he shrugged his shoulders.

"Why are so many people abusing Him and making fun of Him? I heard He only did good things: healing the sick, feeding the hungry, and giving to the needy. Why are they so angry at Him? It doesn't make sense," inquired the man.

"You know how it is. If you threaten the power and authority of some in Israel today, you risk your very life. That is what He has done, and now He pays the price," stated the friend.

"It doesn't seem right that a good man should be treated so," said the man, as he shook his head from side to side in disgust at what was happening.

"He said He was the Messiah, and He said He was the Son of God. That is why they are crucifying Him," cut in another man from the crowd around Him.

"We were just talking about that. Do you think He is?" asked the first man.

"I don't know, but as I look at Him on the Cross, I feel as if my heart is breaking, and I feel as if He is reaching out, putting it back together again," answered the man in the crowd.

"If He was the Messiah, wouldn't He come down from the Cross and show us?" inquired the first man.

"Maybe God wants this to happen. Maybe God wants His Son to die for a reason we do not understand yet," suggested the friend.

"What reason could that be?" asked the first man.

"I don't know, but if it is God's reason, then it will be a very good one," answered the man from the crowd, who had spoken before.

"He is looking at me," said the first man.

"No, He is looking at me," insisted the friend.

"No, it's me He is looking at," said the man in the crowd.

"Maybe He is looking at all of us," said the first man, and the other two nodded in agreement.

"His face is full of pain. Let's say a prayer for Him that His suffering will end soon," suggested the friend.

"His eyes seem to be penetrating my soul," said the first man, as he began to cry.

"And mine," said the friend and the man in the crowd, almost in unison, and then they, too, began to cry.

"Let's pray for Him," sobbed the first man, and then the three crying men offered their tear-filled prayers for the suffering Jesus on the Cross.

As they prayed, their eyes were fixed on the eyes of Jesus, and each one of them felt as if Jesus' love was reaching inside of them and touching their inner being. In unison, the three fell to their knees, and called out softly to Jesus, "Forgive me. I am sorry. Forgive me."

At that moment, Jesus lifted His head and called out, "Father, forgive them. They know not what they do."

The first man said, with his eyes still fixed on Jesus, to the other two, "It is Him. I know He is the Messiah."

The other two, still crying, sobbed, "We know, we know." They remained there crying and staring at Jesus on the Cross; then with all the others present, they heard Jesus call out, "Father, into Your hands, I commend My Spirit."

As Jesus' head dropped and his last breath filled the air, there was silence until the earth shook and the centurion, who was by the Cross, called out in one voice with these three men, "Truly, this was the Son of God!"

A short while later, the first man said to the other two, as they waited near the Cross, looking at Jesus, Who still hung there, "I feel inside me a knowledge that He did this because He loved me. I can't explain it. I just know it is true."

"So do I," agreed the friend. "I know He died for me because He loved me. I feel this is written on my heart; that it is an eternal truth."

The man from the crowd nodded his head saying, "Yes, I feel He died for all of us. How great a love that is. Surely it is the greatest love of all!"